STARTING
YOUR OWN BUSINESS

WHICH?
BOOKS

Published by Consumers' Association

Which? Books are commissioned and researched by
The Association for Consumer Research and published by
Consumers' Association, 2 Marylebone Road,
London NW1 4DF

Distributed by The Penguin Group:
Penguin Books Ltd, 27 Wrights Lane, London W8 5TZ

© 1994 Consumers' Association Ltd
First edition February 1983
revised reprints 1984, 1985
revised editions 1986, 1988
revised reprint November 1989
new edition January 1992
revised edition November 1993
revised edition October 1994

British Library Cataloguing in Publication Data
A catalogue record for this book is available from the British Library

ISBN 0 85202 533 5

This book incorporates changes introduced by the Finance Act 1994.

Cover photographs by courtesy of Sally and Richard Greenhill and
The Geoffrey Goode and Christopher Guy Picture Collection

Typeset by Paston Press Ltd, Loddon, Norfolk
Printed and bound in Great Britain by Richard Clay Limited,
Bungay, Suffolk

STARTING YOUR OWN BUSINESS

CONTENTS

Foreword

Small businesses have become something of a growth industry over the past ten years as more and more people have decided to 'go it alone'. The reasons are many and varied: some people simply want to get out of the rat race and work in the comfort of their own homes; others see working for themselves as a positive step after redundancy; others are entrepreneurs who have never felt happy as employees.

If you are changing from being employed to becoming self-employed, and perhaps, sooner or later, employing others, you will inevitably have to make adjustments to your values and priorities. You will need to be highly motivated, for no one else will push you to achieve your goals; you will also need enthusiasm, commitment and drive. And a flexible approach will help ensure that you can adapt to changes in market conditions. You may also need support from your family because working for yourself is not the same as having a nine-to-five job. Finally, you need to be realistic about what you can achieve and be prepared for hard work.

While many small businesses do succeed, others fail (Dunn and Bradstreet reported that there were 63,000 business failures in 1992). Even some of the successful people probably didn't realise at first just what they were letting themselves in for. To give yourself the best chance of success you need advice and information – not just on the formalities and practicalities but also on the potential pitfalls and difficulties.

A key to success is careful preparation and thought. You will need to investigate your potential market: do you intend to provide a product or service that the public actually wants? To establish this you may want to consult experts and trade organisations, and even undertake a dry run to ensure that your business idea has potential. Are you familiar with your competitors' products and services? Can you provide a better service for your customers?

This book should help you decide what sort of business you want to run and give information about the many organisations which advise. There has never been so much help and encouragement available, so use it. You are likely to have a lot to learn and it is important to learn it quickly so that you can concentrate on building your business.

This book will give you an insight into the things you need to know and the problems you could face; equally importantly, it tells you where to go for more specialised assistance.

CHAPTER 1

HAVING WHAT IT TAKES

TO RUN your own business, of whatever kind, you need not only some capital and some capability but also a certain flair, toughness and some good fortune. Very few of the people who start a small business have enough of both flair and luck to end up as millionaires. You might be one of them; more probably you will succeed in making a living, while enjoying the satisfaction of independence and of doing work you have chosen for yourself.

To achieve this, you must be committed; you must choose a business project that is right for you; and you must prepare yourself as thoroughly as possible before taking the plunge.

Commitment

It is no use being half-hearted when starting up a business: you should be motivated positively, not just negatively by a dislike of the job you are in, or unemployment. Your incentive should be to a large extent financial, and do not set your sights too low: from the start, your aim should be to make a reasonable living.

In becoming your own boss you may find yourself working for a harder taskmaster than any you have had, one who offers unlimited working hours, uncertain holidays and perhaps, to start with, less money than you were earning before. You will be exchanging the support and companionship of fellow workers for a kind of isolation in which you stand or fall by your own decisions.

There will be few executive perks, or none; you will look at these with a different eye when they have to be paid for out of your profits.

The members of your family should feel equally committed. Their moral support, quite apart from any work-support, will be invaluable, especially during periods of difficulty and discouragement. They ought to be aware that their security depends on your success, that you may have less time for family life, and that the rewards may be some time in coming.

Choosing your project

Anyone wanting to start a business has either found a product to manufacture or an idea for one, or has decided to go into distribution, or to provide a service. It is no good saying to yourself, 'I want to go into business but I don't know whether to be a manufacturer or a distributor or to provide a service'.

Your choice of business project is a decision you alone can make, because you are in the best position to know what your marketable skills and capabilities are, and which of them you want to be the foundation of your new career.

You may want to capitalise on the knowledge of a trade, the business training or the managerial experience acquired in your previous work. But if it is work that you are or were unhappy in, you may want to strike out in a new direction.

A hobby which has made you an expert at some trade – for instance, cabinet-making, cooking, dressmaking – can be the start of a business, especially if you have already begun to make money by it in your spare time: you will then have the beginnings of a client list, and some idea of a potential market. When you approach a bank or other organisation for a loan, you will inspire more confidence if you already have some history of successful trading. But remember that it is a big jump from moonlighting to making a living from it, and selling a hobby-item to a few friends and relatives may not be a good indication of its appeal to the general public or of its economic viability.

You may have an original business idea. Perhaps you have designed a new product that fills a gap in the market which everyone else has failed to notice; or you may have an idea for a service which would facilitate the workings of some industry.

You may want to enter an established trade by buying a franchise or into a partnership, or by taking over a going concern.

But if the trade is new to you, be wary; you are unlikely to be able to master it at the same time as learning the complexities of running a business. Bear in mind that you will be competing with people who are already established experts in the field. It is better to get your training and experience first, by working in the trade for a period, and attending any relevant training courses.

Getting off to a flying start

Most businesses have small beginnings which only involve the proprietor in the purchase of premises and equipment. But there are several ways in which the prospective businessperson (and the established businessperson wishing to expand) can take over an existing business or make use of someone else's business idea. This will, in general, involve you in a greater capital outlay, but the right decision can bring with it the knowledge that you have a good chance of making a success of the business. The other side of the coin is that you may risk financial overcommitment or taking on a business which you do not understand adequately.

In making your choice of project (assuming you have a choice), you should define your field of operations as specifically as possible, and be clear about your ultimate aims. If your ambition is to start up a business in one area and then expand elsewhere, or even to build up a great organisation, you must be sure to choose a business that is capable of such growth. If, however, your sole ambition is to make a comfortable living and sell or close down the firm when you retire, do not choose a business which can only survive by continually growing and expanding.

Some ways into your own business
If you have developed an original business idea but do not want to deal with the whole of the business side yourself, you may make an agreement with a manufacturer to make your product, retaining for yourself any part of the operation to which you can offer a unique contribution, such as design or marketing. Do not forget that you should, if possible, protect any truly novel idea (for instance, by applying for a patent), before disclosing it to any interested party.

11

Look around to see if you can find any other small firms, old or new, working in the same or a related field, who might be willing to pool resources with you. For instance, a successful 'merger' of this kind has been achieved between the makers of four-poster beds, piano stools and wooden toys respectively: as well as sharing expenses, they were able to develop a common advertising and marketing policy, while remaining autonomous.

To set up such an arrangement you may have to do plenty of research to find other firms in your line of trade in your locality. Consult the Chamber of Commerce or Chamber of Trade; if there is a Small Business Club, it will probably be willing to advertise your needs among its members. In London, the London Enterprise Agency, 4 Snow Hill, London EC1A 2BS TEL 071-236 3000, has linked up with 12 other enterprise agencies to form a national business introduction service (see also page 23), known as LINC (Local Investment Networking Company Ltd).

Preparation

The decision of when to start will need to be related to the amount of money at your disposal: there is likely to be a period during which you will be paying all the outgoings, with little or no money coming in, while your own living expenses will still have to be met.

Begin by taking stock of your resources and assets, both human and financial. Human assets include your own skills and energy, and those of any member of your family who will be working with you.

Most people starting in business lack one or more of the basic skills needed for success. It is usually cheaper in the long run to buy in a missing skill, say a clerk or bookkeeper, than attempt all the paperwork yourself unless you really know what you are doing. Not only will you take longer than a skilled person and make more mistakes, but spending the same amount of time in using your own skill (selling, for example) will make more money for the business eventually.

Skills to learn

There are certain skills, however, that are worth learning, such as typing, elementary accountancy, computer use, administration. If you intend to have a partner, perhaps your own husband or wife, divide up between you who will learn what, at evening classes perhaps, through books or by correspondence course – quite apart from reading around the main subject of your enterprise.

Get used to the idea that, however knowledgeable you may become in your own field, there is still a lot to learn. And make sure that you take advantage of the various sources of help: a large number of 'Start your own business' training courses are available.

You may find local evening classes that teach basic business skills, or, if you want more advanced training, you can take Open University courses, or short courses at local university or other college business schools.

You may have a One Stop Shop in your area, where you will find advice and information on all aspects of business. At present a few One Stop Shops are in operation, but the initiative is developing to form a network of local business support throughout the country.

The local Training and Enterprise Council (TEC) – Local Enterprise Company (LEC) in Scotland – is a good first point of contact for the small or new entrepreneur. The address of your nearest TEC can be found in the telephone directory.

Each TEC is an independent company, operating under a performance contract with the Government. Their boards of directors are made up primarily of chief executives or managing directors from local businesses, with the remainder being drawn from leaders of education, trade unions, voluntary organisations and the public sector.

The TEC's role is to mobilise business and other interests to establish a strategic approach to raising the levels of education and training ensuring that the necessary skills exist to support a successful economy. TECs also engender enterprising attitudes to support the start-up and development of new businesses.

Working closely with other key business support agencies within their locality, TECs support new and existing small businesses by providing counselling, information, advice and business skills training. Experienced business counsellors offer independent and confidential advice over a wide range of business related matters from preparing a business plan to finding premises, from franchising to exporting and from patents to sources of finance.

The DTI Small Firms Division publishes a variety of free leaflets and booklets, which are available from TECs. One of these leaflets is called *Your Guide to Help for Small Firms*. It provides lots of useful information including sources of help and advice on finance, exporting, innovation and starting a business.

People who have been unemployed may be able to get financial help to launch a new business. The Business Start-up Scheme (formerly the Enterprise Allowance scheme) is run by the TECs and they can set their own conditions, within limits set by the Government. Depending on the local scheme, you could get between £20 and £90 a week, for between 26 and 66 weeks if you have been unemployed for anything from six weeks upwards. For details, contact your local TEC or LEC.

Getting advice

Anyone who has previously always been an employee may find that making decisions without any help is very difficult.

Do not be too proud to ask for advice, preferably from those qualified to give it. You may have friends who are professional people – accountant, bank manager, solicitor – willing to advise you, perhaps initially without charging. Or a friend who is already successfully running his or her own business may be willing to give you the benefit of experience – provided you are not going to be in competition.

Although the bank manager is employed to look after the bank's interest, which may not be the same as your interest, it can be helpful to get his or her opinion, even if the bank is not providing the funds.

It may take months before you can start. You may need to find premises, with all the delays that this involves (including, perhaps, getting planning permission). If your business project is not based on something you are doing already, it is a good idea to make it into a spare-time pursuit while continuing with your job, and thereby getting some valuable experience of the work.

About finance before you start

Whatever your project, you should have a picture in your mind of what stage you intend to have reached in one year's or two years' time, even if you cannot make anything but a very approximate forecast about this. What matters is having a forward plan, against which you will be able to monitor your progress. If things go according to plan, it will give your confidence a boost. And if things are not going as planned, you will be able to take whatever action is necessary.

There are some essential basic concepts you must understand, such as overheads, materials and labour costs, unit costs, start-up capital, working capital, short-term and medium-term finance, cash flow, profit and loss account.

The cost of producing anything is made up of a number of elements; how many are involved depends on whether it is a product or a service. Reduced to their simplest terms, they are as follows:

Cost of materials
These are materials from which products are made. The cost of materials in one year, divided by the number of units of the product manufactured in that year, gives the materials cost per unit.

For a retailer or wholesaler, the materials are the stock of goods. An agent or consultant has no materials costs.

Overheads
Generally speaking, these are the standing costs of the business which must be paid whether or not you succeed in making and selling anything.

In the annual accounts, overheads are classified under the following headings:

Salaries and wages	before-tax remuneration paid to office and sales staff, also directors' salaries and any other money drawn out of the business
Rent and rates	
Heating, lighting and other services	gas, electricity, oil, propane gas, water and sewerage, etc
Advertising/marketing	(excluding the cost of any special launch)
Printing, postage and stationery, telephone, fax	all office supplies and expenses
Motor and travel expenses	tax, insurance, servicing and repairs, petrol; expenses of travel by other means
Leasing and/or hire charges	
Insurances	
Professional fees	accountant, solicitor, patent agent
Depreciation	including motor vehicles
Interest on loans and overdraft	rough estimate
Sundry expenses	

Every single one of the overheads costs must be allowed for when you are working out what to charge for a unit of your product or an hour of your time. If you underestimate your overheads, you may find that far from making a profit, you are actually working at a loss.

Direct labour costs

In a manufacturing business, these are the before-tax wages paid to the people who actually make the product (not the wages of ancillary workers such as sales and office staff).

To find the labour cost per unit, divide the total annual labour costs by the number of product units.

In practice, labour costs should be considered as overheads, since they are fixed: you cannot as a rule hire workers when you have orders for your product, and lay them off when you have none.

Costing your products

Estimate, pessimistically, how many units of your product you will make and sell in your first year of full production, given your present resources. Work out the total overheads cost for this period. By dividing the second figure by the first, you get the overheads cost per unit. Thus, if the estimated production is 10,000 units and total overheads are £20,000, you must add £2 to the materials and labour cost of each unit, to break even.

But, of course, you want to do better than just cover your costs, so you add to your break-even figure an amount which will be your profit.

Costing in a service industry

The principle is similar, except that instead of charging per unit of product, you will charge per hour of the time spent by a member of your staff in actually doing a job. Overheads usually represent the chief element of costs of the business. If you are, for instance, a washing-machine engineer, or a plumber, your charge for an hour of time should include travelling time and expenses, the cost of tools and equipment, and the wages of the person who answers the telephone and makes out the invoices: all these are overheads. And the chief element in the overheads will be salaries or wages which have to be paid whether or not anyone is actually out on a job. To all this you must add your profit charge. When you do a job yourself, you should also charge for your time, and include a profit element.

If your total overheads costs come to £8,000 for an estimated total of 1,000 job-hours per year, your break-even price per hour will be £8. If you have to replace the washing-machine's drum or motor, you will have to charge the customer separately for materials.

What is start-up capital?

This is the 'once-for-all' expenditure needed to start a new business, the cash you must lay out before you have manufactured a single item, or dealt with a single client. Unless you start off in your garage with a second-hand typewriter, you will have to pay for some, though not necessarily all, of the following:

- premises: buying or rebuilding, conversion or even building from scratch
- plant and equipment, tools
- goodwill, if taking over an existing business
- office equipment and furniture
- installation of electricity, gas, telephone and any other services
- initial administrative costs: legal and other professional fees
- stationery: the paper, envelopes, postcards, invoices, etc printed with the firm's name
- publicity: cost of the initial launch
- insurance: for equipment, premises, liability, for instance, public and employers'.

You should assess this expenditure as accurately as possible and consider ways of reducing it if necessary (for instance, by delaying the buying of any pieces of plant not immediately needed, or by leasing or hiring plant instead of buying).

When you begin to work out how much money you are going to need for your project, you must be sure to include not only the start-up capital (the money needed to get your business going) but also the working capital (the money you need to keep you going during the interval between paying for your outgoings and claiming for your receipts).

What is working capital?

In a manufacturing industry, once production starts, some weeks or even months must pass before the products are finished, sold, despatched and paid for. In the meantime, you must keep paying for materials, labour and overheads: the cost of all of these represents your working capital needs.

If you need to keep large stocks of raw materials or finished products or have a number of people on the payroll, materials costs and labour costs will be tied up without, for the time being, any returns. Your working capital will therefore need to be so much the greater. If your suppliers give you 30 days' credit, and your customers pay cash in seven days (in return for a small discount, perhaps), your working capital requirement will be reduced. At the same time, you will speed up your cash flow, that is, the rate at which money passes out of and into your business. Working capital and cash flow are closely related: the more money you have lying stagnant – in materials, stock, or in customers' unpaid invoices – the more working capital you will need.

In the retail and distributive trades (that is, a shop), where the goods held in stock represent the materials costs, the amount of working capital needed and the rate of cash flow depend on the amount of unsold stock, not so much on unpaid invoices because the retail trade has the advantage that customers generally pay straightaway. A service industry, without stocks of materials or direct labour costs, needs comparatively little working capital: enough to pay overheads costs till the money starts coming in.

Short-term finance
As the name suggests, it is money required for short periods of time. It may be needed for start-up capital or for temporary increases in working capital.

If you are setting up a service business or an agency, or plan to be a middleman rather than a manufacturer, you may need little in the way of plant and labour, and consequently a comparatively small start-up capital. But you may still need short-term money, to cover the interval between your outgoings and your receipts.

Such short-term finance can be in the form of a loan for a stated amount, generally with a fixed interest rate and repayment date, or an overdraft. An overdraft usually has a top limit beyond which you cannot borrow; interest is calculated on a daily basis and varies according to the prevailing base rate. An overdraft is usually one of the cheapest forms of borrowing even though there may be a setting-up charge. Its great disadvantage is that it is repayable on demand – though banks seldom call it in over the short term, as timing will usually have been agreed in advance.

Medium-term finance

This is money repayable in three to seven years, and is usually needed as start-up capital to pay for plant and equipment, but it may be working capital. In the past, it was possible to borrow at a fixed rate of interest, but now, with frequent fluctuations in the base rate, a variable rate is common. The fixed-rate loan, if you can get it, is something of a gamble – you stand to lose if interest rates fall – but it does give the advantage of stability: you know exactly how much you will have to pay for your loan, which is a help in making estimates. It is generally possible to repay a loan before it is due and you must be able to pay off the full amount by the stated date.

CHAPTER 2

WHERE TO GO FOR MONEY AND ADVICE

BY AND LARGE, money will always be forthcoming for a sound project if well presented. If you cannot get money for your project, either there is some flaw in it, or you have not presented it to the best advantage. If you ask your bank manager for a loan or overdraft on the basis of a few figures on the back of an envelope, you will scarcely inspire confidence.

The most obvious source of finance is a bank. Buying money is not very different from buying anything else. Banks make their profits from lending money and they want your business, provided they are sure they will not lose by it. It is best to approach your own bank in the first instance; the manager knows the state of your account, and if you are generally solvent and in control of your outgoings, this will give the bank some confidence in you. You may get a rapid response, but if you do not, rather than just waiting for the answer which may turn out to be 'no', approach two or three other commercial institutions.

Where the money may come from

If your own high-street bank refuses, try the other clearing banks, any of which may provide the finance. There are also numerous merchant banks able to provide medium-term finance. If your project is closely associated with another country, an approach to one of the country's banks might bring results.

Many banks have developed special schemes for helping new businesses: they include unsecured loan schemes, and loans with capital repayment deferred. It is therefore worthwhile to investigate various banks as possible sources.

3i

Another line of attack is provided by 3i plc (investors in industry), jointly owned by the Bank of England and the English and Scottish clearing banks. 3i invests in businesses across the whole business spectrum, from family firms to high-technology enterprises. It helps them at all stages of change: at start-up, when risk capital may be required; during expansion; and during later phases of development, such as diversification, acquisition, management buy-out and management buy-in. Where there is a risk element, 3i subscribes for a minority share in the business, in recognition of its role in sharing the risk.

Contact 3i at 91 Waterloo Road, London SE1 8XP   TEL 071-928 3131 for the address of your local area office.

British Technology Group (BTG)

British Technology Group's objective is to promote the development and commercial use of new technology arising from research. BTG searches for new technology and products in laboratories and companies worldwide; protects these technologies through effective patenting and enforcement; can provide funding, where necessary, for further developmental work; and negotiates licences with industrial companies on an international basis.

BTG covers all aspects of licensing, which include technology and commercial appraisal, patenting, legal, finance, marketing, negotiating, revenue collection and auditing.

BTG holds more than 10,000 patents and patent applications covering over 1,600 technologies.

Further information can be obtained from the Director of Corporate Communications, British Technology Group, 101 Newington Causeway, London SE1 6BU   TEL 071-403 6666.

How to find an investor

There are several agencies which can put you in touch with people with funds to invest.

LINC

LINC (Local Investment Networking Company Ltd) puts entrepreneurs seeking finance in touch with potential investors who may also have the management skills to put into the business. It consists of 12 agencies:

- Barfield Enterprise Training   TEL 081-447 9422
- Glasgow Opportunities (MidWest Scottish Consortium) TEL 041-221 0955
- Great Western Enterprise Ltd   TEL (0793) 514055
- London Enterprise Agency (LEntA), 4 Snow Hill, London EC1A 2BS   TEL 071-236 3000
- Medway Enterprise Agency Ltd   TEL (0634) 366565
- Northamptonshire Enterprise Agency   TEL (0604) 37401/2
- North Derbyshire Enterprise Agency   TEL (0246) 207379
- Sheffield Enterprise Agency   TEL (0742) 755721
- Somerset Enterprise Services Ltd   TEL (0823) 323515
- Staffordshire Development Association   TEL (0785) 51449
- TechInvest   TEL (0606) 737009
- West Cornwall Enterprise Ltd   TEL (0209) 714914.

More than 250 other enterprise agencies throughout the country also undertake this 'marriage-bureau' function.

BVCA

The British Venture Capital Association (BVCA) is the trade association for the UK venture capital industry. It combines the role of a representative voice for Britain's venture capitalists with the role of putting those seeking venture capital in touch with those who provide it. Members of BVCA normally take minority stakes in companies, by participating in management through representation on the board of directors. This allows them to have a continuing involvement with their investees, and to help entrepreneurs and managers to obtain maximum performance, and to increase the value of the companies.

Members' names can be found in the Association's annual directory, which gives company details, as well as the detailed investment criteria for each member: minimum investment, preferred investment, type of funding, stage of investment, investment conditions, industry and geographical preferences. Copies of the directory can be obtained from the BVCA at 3 Catherine Place, London SW1E 6DX   TEL 071-233 5212.

The Association does not recommend individual members, and suggests that you choose, from the directory, members offering funds and conditions appropriate to your particular financing requirements, and contact them directly.

Enterprise Investment Scheme (EIS)

After ten years, the Business Expansion Scheme (BES) has been retired and replaced with the EIS. Like the BES, the EIS is designed to attract individuals to invest relatively small amounts of capital in unquoted businesses. It works by giving investors tax relief when they purchase newly issued full-risk shares in an unquoted trading company. Unlike the BES, companies trading in the UK are eligible for the EIS even if they are not incorporated or resident there. Another important difference between the BES and the EIS is that investors can become paid directors of the company provided they had not been linked to the company before the shares were issued. The scheme is not open to employees or shareholders with over 30 per cent of the shares.

An investor is able to obtain income tax relief at the lower tax rate (20 per cent in 1994–5) on up to £100,000 of investment in any one tax year. If the qualifying conditions are met, the proceeds arising from the disposal of the shares after five years or more are exempt from capital gains tax. If the shares realise a loss at that time, relief against income tax or capital gains tax can be claimed.

A company can raise a maximum of £1 million through the EIS in any one tax year. A higher limit of £5 million applies to companies engaged in certain shipping activities. Companies trading in private rented housing (which were covered by the BES) are specifically excluded from the EIS.

If you are in any doubt about whether your company qualifies for the EIS, you should consult your accountant or tax inspector.

Other possibilities

Ask any contact you may have in the world of finance – your bank manager, accountant, stockbroker, if you have one – whether they know of anybody looking for an investment. Some people have found investors by advertising in the personal columns of the daily press, but do not hope for too much with this method.

Help depending on location

The Government has designated certain areas of Britain as 'assisted areas', in which it is anxious to create employment. These are subdivided into development and intermediate areas, and two new schemes of assistance grants have been introduced specifically for their benefit. You cannot receive both types of regional grant for the same project. And it is very important that you should apply for assistance before you embark on a project, and not afterwards: once you have started, you may find it very hard to prove to the DTI that you need their help.

Regional Enterprise Grants

Regional Enterprise Grants (REG) are available towards investment and innovation projects in most manufacturing and some service industries.

Investment grants are available in Development Areas, the Intermediate Areas in Derbyshire, South Yorkshire, Plymouth and Fife (as part of the European Regional Development Fund) and in localities affected by colliery closures, to companies with fewer than 25 employees (full-time equivalent) worldwide. Investment projects may receive 15 per cent grants on expenditure on eligible fixed assets in the project up to a maximum grant of £15,000; eligible expenditure includes plant and machinery (new or second-hand), buildings, purchase of land and site preparation and vehicles used solely on site.

Innovation grants are available in Development, Intermediate, EC Objective 2, Task Force and City Challenge Areas, localities affected by colliery closures and certain Scottish urban areas to companies with fewer than 50 employees (full-time equivalent) worldwide. Innovation projects which lead to the development and introduction of new products and processes may be granted 50 per cent of eligible costs, up to a maximum of £25,000. The project must be innovative to the applicant and involve technical risk.

A brochure which includes guidance notes and an application form is available from the Department of Trade and Industry, Regional Development and Inward Investment Division, Room 332 Kingsgate House, 66–74 Victoria Street, London SW1E 6SW   TEL 071-215 8459.

Regional selective assistance

This is available in both kinds of assisted area, for projects both in manufacturing and service industries. Project grants are based on the fixed capital costs of a project, and on the number of jobs the project is expected to create or safeguard. The level of grant is negotiated as the minimum necessary for the project to proceed. Projects should have a good chance of paying their way, and should contribute both to the regional and the national benefit.

A booklet, entitled *The Regional Initiative – Guide to Regional Selective Assistance*, is available from the Department of Trade and Industry, Investment, Development and Accountancy Services Division, Room 233, Kingsgate House, 66–74 Victoria Street, London SW1E 6SW   TEL 071-215 2565.

The Rural Development Commission offers advice and loans to applicants who employ fewer than 20 skilled people. The loans are for buildings, equipment and also working capital. The minimum loan is £250, the maximum is £75,000, but the loan is never more than 50 per cent of the cost of the particular project. Interest is payable on the loan at a rate slightly lower than that charged by the commercial market.

In rural development areas, the Rural Development Commission can help businesses to obtain a 25 per cent grant towards the cost of converting buildings to new job-creating uses. Some of the other services on offer are these: on-the-job skill training in a wide range of trades; help in finding premises; technical building advice, and help with planning permission. The Commission's management accountants and marketing officers will advise on drawing up profit plans and marketing plans. The Rural Development Commission also operates joint schemes with some of the major banks, which makes larger loans available.

There are some 25 local offices which help with technical or management problems of a small business in rural areas, also including towns of up to 10,000 inhabitants. Further information can be obtained from:

- England   Rural Development Commission, 141 Castle Street, Salisbury, Wiltshire SP1 3TP   TEL (0722) 336255
- Wales   Business Development Unit of the Welsh Development Agency, Business Development Centre, Treforest Industrial Estate, Pontypridd, Mid Glamorgan CF37 5UR   TEL (0443) 841777
- Scotland   Lothian and Edinburgh Enterprises Ltd (LEEL), Apex House, Haymarket Terrace, Edinburgh EH12 5HD   TEL 031-313 4000
- Northern Ireland   LEDU, LEDU House, Upper Galwally, Belfast BT8 4TB   TEL (0232) 491031.

London has Greater London Enterprise (GLE), an investment and business development agency owned by thirteen London boroughs. GLE works with the private sector to provide venture capital for small and medium-sized businesses, with the aim of creating more and better quality employment in the London area. GLE provides a comprehensive range of business development and property services, and has its own Enterprise Training Centre which runs a variety of courses and seminars. For details and conditions contact GLE, 63–67 Newington Causeway, London SE1 6BD   TEL 071–403 0300.

In some of the major cities too, local authorities have created similar support agencies. These are administered by the Department of the Environment, through the local authorities, making grants or loans to help buy land or renovate buildings, etc.

Some of the grants mentioned here may be taxable, so you should ask about this at an early stage.

Enterprise Initiative

The DTI's Enterprise Initiative aims to provide the tools to help businesses take full advantage of market opportunities by providing practical help and guidance in several areas such as strategic management advice, exports, technology and regional development.

An important element of the Enterprise Initiative is the Consultancy Scheme, which encourages the use of outside expertise as a regular part of management strategy. The Scheme provides financial support, in the form of a subsidy, to help firms tackle a number of management projects covering six key management areas; quality, marketing, design, manufacturing and services systems, financial and management information systems and business planning. Consultancy help is available to most independent firms or groups with fewer than 500 employees.

Grants are also available through the following schemes: Small Firms Merit Award for Research and Technology (SMART), Support for Product Under Research (SPUR), Regional Enterprise Grants, which are available for investment and innovation, and Regional Selective Assistance, which is the principle instrument of regional industrial policy.

For more information, get the free DTI booklet, *The Enterprise Initiative*, which lists all the DTI's regional contact points. Freephone (0800) 500200 or contact the DTI Enterprise Initiative Division, Kingsgate House, 66–74 Victoria Street, London SW1E 6SJ   TEL 071-215 8379.

Presenting your case

Government help, or local government help, is by no means automatically available even where such stipulations as the creation of fresh employment are met. One prerequisite in all cases is that the proposed business must show itself likely to be viable.

In some cases it is stipulated that the presentation of a proposal must conform to a standard form, which may include an independent accountant's report. Each organisation has its own set of rules, so the proposal should be written to satisfy these rules. The information that the funding organisations need, and the way it is presented, should be very carefully prepared: it is almost a professional task. It is probably worth involving an accountant at this stage, if only to help you present a cash flow forecast.

The Rural Development Commission offers help in drawing up funding propositions for presentation to the bank.

The bank itself may help you with a cash flow forecast: all the major banks run some form of business advisory service, free to customers, but this help is mainly intended for established businesses. However, many of the banks publish booklets intended for the person who wants to start a business.

The local enterprise agency is a good first point of contact for the small or new entrepreneur, and everyone in the United Kingdom lives within 30 miles of one of these agencies. The address and telephone number of your nearest agency can be found by telephoning 071-629 1600.

Local enterprise agencies are supported by partnerships between local industry and local and central government. They are independent organisations, nearly all run by experienced business people, offering free confidential counselling to people wishing to start a business. They can advise – or, if necessary, suggest other advisers – on problems to do with the sources of finance, and with marketing, planning and training, and finding premises. They may run a number of other initiatives to support local small businesses, such as business training and seminars, small business clubs, and managed small workshop units. 'Managed' means that a manager, who may be employed by the enterprise agency or seconded from a company, attends to the letting of the units and the provision of facilities, and is also available to help and advise the tenants.

In London, the activities of LEntA, the London Enterprise Agency, include a training programme with one-day conferences giving an introduction to the basic requirements for starting and running a business, or an advanced course of four linked weekends. There is also a counselling service dealing with finance which also helps in presenting a case to providers of finance; it also gives advice on marketing strategy and research, and assists with patents, technical problems and the commercial aspects of developing an innovation.

Whoever helps you present your case, make sure that you, yourself, understand and believe in the assumptions and the calculations, because it is you who will have to explain and justify them to the bank manager or other potential lender, and it will be your responsibility to produce the results to match them. Your forecast must demonstrate not only that you have coherent and realistic plans for the future, but also that you will be monitoring your progress against them, week by week, month by month, and are unlikely to be overwhelmed by unforeseen disasters.

What the bank manager wants to know

Make an appointment and say why you want to see the bank manager. If you are a customer, the manager will want to look up your banking record before the appointment to be assured that you can handle your money responsibly. A past overdraft will not be held against you. If you are not a customer, references from your own bank will be asked for.

The bank manager will want to know what kind of business you intend to set up; what kind and size of market you expect to trade in; the likely extent of the competition; how you propose to go about marketing your product. He or she will ask why you consider yourself particularly qualified for this business; whether you have experience of it, for how long and with what success; and whether you have sought expert advice.

The bank manager will, perhaps surprisingly, want to be sure that you are not asking for too little money. Many beginners in business are too modest in their requirements: they do not take account of all the overheads to be paid for, and forget to make provision for slack times in the trade, or unforeseen contingencies, such as a dock strike affecting export business. So, if in doubt, ask for more rather than less.

Offering security

The question of what security you can offer is bound to arise. A bank may lend without it, but only on an exceptionally sound proposition, and not always then.

A life insurance policy is unlikely to bring in much if you surrender it to provide capital for your business, but it may be acceptable as security for a bank loan. If you own a house or other real estate, you can use it as security for a loan or overdraft, provided that it is freehold, or on a long lease (over 21 years left, say) but the bank's estimate of its value will certainly be a good deal lower than yours, even after you deduct the amount owing on a first mortgage.

An alternative to consider would be selling your house and moving to a cheaper one, or a rented one, to provide more start-up capital. If you intend to buy or rent a factory from a local authority, especially in a development area, this may secure you a high place on the housing list.

You may feel that to part with the roof over the family's head is too rash, but the people you will be asking for a loan will expect you to carry a portion of the risk. It is important to know that most financial organisations will expect your own stake in the business to equal theirs.

There is a loan guarantee scheme which helps small businesses to raise loans from banks and some commercial sources where a loan would not have been granted without such guarantee. The Department of Trade and Industry, through its Small Business Loan Guarantee Scheme, may guarantee up to 70 per cent of a loan of not more than £100,000 for new business and 85 per cent of a loan of up to £250,000 for established businesses. The 85 per cent guarantee is also available for new or established businesses based in any of the City Task Force or City Challenge Areas.

In either case, the applicant must be willing to pledge all available business assets as security for the guaranteed loan, and must already have committed all personal assets (including his or her home) to secure conventional term loans or overdrafts. A premium is charged for the guarantee by the DTI. The premium rate at present is 1.5 per cent per annum for variable rate lending or 0.5 per cent on fixed rate lending on the whole amount of the loan. In all cases, the commercial decisions affecting the borrower are taken by the lender; the DTI cannot intervene.

For loans up to £30,000, a simplified scheme called Small Loans Arrangement operates. It means that the major participating banks can approve loan applications without having first to refer them to the DTI, which speeds up lending decisions.

Full information about this scheme can be obtained from your local TEC or LEC, or from the Loan Guarantee Unit of the Department of Trade and Industry, Small Firms Division, Level 2, St Mary's House, c/o Moorfoot, Sheffield S1 4PQ   TEL (0742) 597308/9.

It is very easy, in the excitement of trying to raise capital for a project about which you are very enthusiastic, to give too much security to your source of finance, leaving nothing for future borrowing.

One other point: banks and other financial institutions usually make a charge for setting up a loan arrangement, generally of the order of at least 1 per cent (negotiated individually in each case). This should be allowed for in your planning calculations.

The bank manager or other potential lender will want to know exactly what resources you have, which may include redundancy money, savings, stocks and shares and other securities and investments, valuables convertible into cash; and the value of your house and car. He or she will want to know where the rest of the financing of your enterprise will come from (including other loans, perhaps a loan from a member of the family, at low interest). He or she will want to know how much you want to borrow, for how long and how you propose to pay it back, and will want to see a budget and a cash flow forecast for at least 12 months which will demonstrate that the loan can be repaid.

Cash flow forecasting

At any given time there will be a difference between your outgoings and your receipts, which has to be covered from funds available in reserve, or by bank overdraft or other forms of credit.

Cash flow forecasting is calculating what this difference will be, based on month by month predictions (or educated guesses) about the times when you will be paying out and when you will be collecting money, over a period of, say, six months or a year.

The outgoings, which are largely predictable, include wages (the payment of which can never be postponed), and materials (remember that some suppliers insist on cash on delivery), VAT (which is normally paid quarterly and is refunded to you quarterly, so it is also a reliable source of receipts) and overheads.

Your overheads will include major bills payable at different intervals: insurance once a year, rent, electricity, gas, telephone once a quarter, and so on. All these will be entered in the books as they are paid, making for an irregular pattern in your accounting, with several bills in some months, and none in others.

Receipts

The calculation of receipts is less predictable. The level of sales is likely to fluctuate from month to month. Some customers pay cash in seven days, usually expecting to be rewarded by a cash discount (negotiated in advance), others pay in 30 or 60 days (also by previous arrangement). There are bad customers and bad debts, so that part of your money may be outstanding for a long time – or forever: you should allow an estimated sum for this in each month's calculations of receipts.

It is because outgoings are more predictable than receipts that cash flow forecasting is so essential, right from the start: you may have to provide funds for wages, materials and overheads for some months during which there is little or nothing coming in.

The cash flow forecast indicates the actual movement of money, not promises to pay: it is concerned strictly with what comes in and goes out, and the time of each transaction. If you intend to raise capital by borrowing from a bank, the manager will want to examine your cash flow forecast in order to assess your ability to control your financial resources. And your bank manager will also want to see a profit and loss forecast.

How to set up a profit and loss forecast

Start by choosing a target: the amount of sales you think you can achieve in one year's time. Use as the break-even figure the minimum amount you need for your business and personal expenses, and decide how soon you have to reach that point. Not till then is the business moving into profit.

Your sales will need to increase steadily month by month in order to reach the target figure on time. Work out a set of projected monthly sales figures, and arrange them on a 12-month table.

A practical example, using manufactured products to set out the various problems, is that of Bill, a newly started small-scale manufacturer (but exactly the same method would be used for any other kind of business).

Bill, who is ambitious and confident of his market, plans to achieve sales of £50,000 a month by the end of the first year, so he plans his first year's sales as in line (1) in table A (see page 35).

VAT does not directly affect the calculation of business profits, so Bill disregards it in this forecast on both sales and purchases.

Bill enters in line (2) his cost of materials, which he estimates as a percentage (namely 50 per cent) of sales. He plans to use part-time labour in the first instance, building up to full-time employees as and when they can be justified. His labour figures, again a rough estimate, are expressed in line (3) as a percentage of sales (namely 30 per cent).

By subtracting the labour and materials costs from the receipts, Bill finds his monthly gross profit, in line (4).

In the case of a single-handed owner in a small service industry – say, a plumber – there would be no labour and materials costs, all expenses being charged as overheads, and the sales figures would also be the gross profit figures. In a retail or wholesale business, the materials would be the purchases of stock.

Bill knows that his overheads will vary from month to month; he is doing a one-year profit forecast, and so it is legitimate to average them over 12 months, in line (5).

The resulting set of figures in line (6) is the monthly net profit, and shows him that after the business has broken even at month 6, it is notionally trading at a profit.

Bill realises that if the business borrows money, then the interest charges will reduce the net profit, and he will need to amend the forecast.

He also realises that because he is the owner of the business as 'sole trader' (not a company), he cannot claim his monthly drawings (for his own living expenses) as a salary, that is, as part of the firm's overheads. He will need to discuss his drawings with his bank manager. If he were trading as a limited company, he

TABLE A

Bill's projected profit and loss account (*figures in £'s 000, those in square brackets are deficit*)

month	1	2	3	4	5	6	7	8	9	10	11	12	Total	% of sales
(1) sales receipts	1	3	6	10	15	20	25	30	35	40	45	50	280	100
(2) *less* materials purchased	0.5	1.5	3	5	7.5	10	12.5	15	17.5	20	22.5	25	140	50
(3) *less* direct labour	0.3	0.9	1.8	3	4.5	6	7.5	9	10.5	12	13.5	15	84	30
(4) gross profit	0.2	0.6	1.2	2	3	4	5	6	7	8	9	10	56	20
(5) overheads	4	4	4	4	4	4	4	4	4	4	4	4	48	17
(6) net profit	[3.8]	[3.4]	[2.8]	[2.0]	[1.0]	–	1	2	3	4	5	6	8	3

would pay himself a director's salary, and that would be included in the overheads.

The next step

Estimating profits is, however, only half of the story. The second, and more important half, is being in control of the cash flow. However much profit you expect to be making by the end of the first year, your estimates will be in vain if in the meantime you cannot meet your suppliers' invoices, or your overhead expenses – not to mention the living expenses of you and your family.

How to set up a cash flow forecast

Table B (see page 37) shows how Bill works out his cash flow forecast.

He reckons that he needs about £15,000 to buy plant, machinery and office furnishing. He plans to sell his present car (and lease a small van). This, with his redundancy money, means that he has some £7,000 in the bank. He has persuaded his father-in-law to let him have a further £5,000 if it is required, as a stand-by interest-free loan, to be repaid from profits.

He bases his calculations on the same 12-month scheme as his profit and loss forecast, entering his £7,000 in line (8) in the first month. It is personal capital paid into the business.

He estimates his monthly payments to suppliers in line (2): they are the materials costs from his profit forecast, and must be paid in cash, as Bill has not yet become creditworthy. He is charged VAT on these costs.

For line (3) Bill reckons that he can spread his capital payments (for plant and machinery) over the first six months during which time he will be building up his sales. He is charged VAT on these purchases.

Wages and salaries (including National Insurance contributions) in line (4) must be paid promptly.

For the purpose of costing, the overheads were averaged out per unit of product, but they cannot be averaged out in making a cash flow forecast: the bills come in and have to be paid at irregular intervals, and this is reflected in line (5). VAT will be

TABLE B

Bill's projected cash flow (figures in £'s 000, those in square brackets are deficit)

month	1	2	3	4	5	6	7	8	9	10	11	12	13
(1) opening bank balance/ overdraft	nil	[2.18]	[10.72]	[19.9]	[26.06]	[30.56]	[38.56]	[47.69]	[46.12]	[46.11]	[53.0]	[47.12]	[42.12]
PAYMENTS (inc VAT)													
(2) suppliers	0.59	1.76	3.53	5.88	8.81	11.75	14.69	17.63	20.56	23.5	26.44	29.38	29.38
(3) plant & machinery	2.35	5.88	2.35	1.18	2.35	3.53							
(4) wages & salaries (inc NI)	0.3	0.9	1.8	3.0	4.5	6.0	7.5	9.0	10.5	12.0	13.5	15.0	15.0
(5) overheads with VAT	2.94	1.18	3.53		0.59	2.35		1.18	1.18		1.18		
no VAT	8.0		1.5	5.0		2.0	8.0		3.0	5.0		3.5	8.0
(6) VAT office							2.44			7.52			11.63
(7) maximum borrowing requirement	[14.18]	[11.9]	[23.43]	[34.96]	[42.31]	[56.19]	[71.19]	[75.5]	[81.36]	[94.13]	[94.12]	[95.0]	[106.13]
RECEIPTS (inc VAT)													
(8) capital – Bill	7.0												
– family loan	5.0												
(9) sales	–	1.18	3.53	7.05	11.75	17.63	23.5	29.38	35.25	41.13	47.0	52.88	58.75
(10) VAT office				1.85									
Closing bank balance (11) projected borrowing	[2.18]	[10.72]	[19.9]	[26.06]	[30.56]	[38.56]	[47.69]	[46.12]	[46.11]	[53.0]	[47.12]	[42.12]	[47.38]

charged on some overheads (e.g., advertising, stationery) but not on others (e.g., rent and rates). Bill includes the appropriate amounts.

It is obvious to Bill that he will need his father-in-law's loan, so he includes it in line (8).

Bill next goes to line (9) and fills in his sales figures (including VAT), but, as he is giving a month's credit, his first cash receipts come in month 2. He now deals with VAT in lines (6) and (10). He totals the VAT charged against the business in each quarter: against this he sets the corresponding amounts which he has charged against his customers. But the VAT office (HM Customs and Excise) does not recognise the one month's credit he gives to his customers so, for VAT purposes, Bill must carry back the sales receipt figures to the month before: e.g., the sales credited in month 2 represent a VAT receipt in month 1, in which the goods were invoiced and delivered. In months 1–3, more VAT has been charged against the business than the business has charged, so Bill gets a refund from the VAT office in month 4 (line 10). The case is altered in the subsequent quarters, and Bill has to pass on the excess received to the VAT office, line (6).

Bill now looks at the cash flow month by month. For month 1, the total of payments which is the maximum borrowing requirement (line 7), exceeds both his capital and the family loan (line 8), leaving the business with an overdraft of £2,180 (line 1). He carries this forward as the opening figure in line 1 for month 2. By the end of month 2, the overdraft has increased to £10,720, even with the receipts from the first month's sales. This, too, is carried forward to line 1 for month 3, and so on, month by month. Bill's borrowing requirement, line (11), increases and, at the end of the year, his overdraft is over £42,000, and has been even higher than this for the previous five months.

Bill is startled to find that he needs such heavy borrowing to achieve a profit of £8,000 (net, but before interest payments) for the year. This is daunting; he notices that the borrowing drops after reaching a peak in month 10, and this looks to be a promising trend. To check this, he adds a month 13 projection, keeping purchases from suppliers steady at the month 12 level. Alas, he finds that his overdraft increases again because of the VAT payment he has to make in this month. He then looks to see if there are any overheads which he can re-time, or delay paying, but finds that this makes no significant difference to his business.

To improve his cash flow forecast, Bill looks at ways of reducing all outgoings. He accepts that reduced purchases of materials will necessarily reduce sales. He fixes on a less ambitious sales figure of £40,000, but aims for a faster growth in sales, so that he will achieve that figure in month 10, and break even in month 5. By leasing instead of buying some of the plant and machinery he can reduce his capital cash expenditure, but will incur leasing charges, on which VAT is payable. He needs to re-time some of the outgoings, but feels it would be unwise to reduce them all.

Bill now amends his profit and loss forecast, and his cash flow forecast, as shown in tables C and D. Table C shows profits only £200 lower, and table D shows reduced borrowing from month 7. The year-end overdraft is now £23,230, nearly £19,000 down on his first forecast. He finds that in month 13 the overdraft increases, but is still nearly £18,000 down on the original forecast.

The new forecasts, like the old ones, do not provide for interest on borrowing, or for Bill's personal drawings. None of them answers the question: 'When can you repay the loan?' which the lenders are sure to ask. Bill does a back-of-the-envelope extension forecast to month 24: he assumes no changes in purchases and sales, wages, overheads, etc., and ignores inflation. He realises that this is very rough and ready and unrealistic, but still, by showing the cash flow in credit for the last few months, it is a pointer to the sort of term which Bill needs for his borrowing, i.e. 3–5 years, rather than 15–20 years.

Bill believes that the new forecasts can be met, and that they can serve as the foundation of a preliminary talk with the bank manager. After that, they will have to be worked up, probably with professional help, before being presented to the bank or to other possible lenders.

Not borrowing but leasing

Leasing is a form of getting medium-term finance without the need to borrow money. The plant, equipment and vehicles you

TABLE C

Bill's amended projected profit and loss account (*figures in £'s 000, those in square brackets are deficit*)

month	1	2	3	4	5	6	7	8	9	10	11	12	Total	% of sales
(1) sales receipts less VAT	3	6	10	15	20	25	30	35	35	40	40	40	299	100
(2) *less* materials purchased	1.5	3	5	7.5	10	12.5	15	17.5	17.5	20	20	20	149.5	50
(3) *less* direct labour	0.9	1.8	3.0	4.5	6.0	7.5	9.0	10.5	10.5	12	12	12	89.7	30
(4) gross profit	0.6	1.2	2.0	3.0	4.0	5.0	6.0	7.0	7.0	8.0	8.0	8.0	59.8	20
(5) overheads	4	4	5	4	4	5	4	4	5	4	4	5	52.0	17.3
(6) net profit	[3.4]	[2.8]	[3.0]	[1.0]	—	—	2	3	2	4	4	3	7.8	2.7

TABLE D

Bill's amended projected cash flow (*figures in £'s 000, those in square brackets are deficit*)

month	1	2	3	4	5	6	7	8	9	10	11	12	13
(1) opening bank balance/ overdraft	nil	[4.54]	[8.7]	[19.59]	[26.69]	[28.57]	[30.44]	[40.33]	[36.73]	[32.02]	[39.7]	[30.55]	[23.23]
PAYMENTS (inc VAT)													
(2) suppliers	1.76	3.53	5.88	8.81	11.75	14.69	17.63	20.56	20.56	23.5	23.5	23.5	23.5
(3) plant & machinery	2.35	1.18	2.35	1.18									
(4) wages & salaries (inc NI)	0.9	1.8	3.0	4.5	6.0	7.5	9.0	10.5	10.5	12.0	12.0	12.0	12.0
(5) overheads – with VAT	3.53	1.18	3.53		1.76			0.59	1.18				
– no VAT	8.0		2.0	5.0		2.0	8.0		3.0	5.0		3.0	8.0
– leasing			1.18			1.18			1.18		2.35	1.18	
(6) VAT office							4.64			8.31			9.97
(7) maximum borrowing requirement	[16.54]	[12.23]	[26.64]	[39.08]	[46.2]	[53.94]	[69.71]	[71.98]	[73.15]	[80.83]	[77.55]	[70.23]	[76.7]
RECEIPTS (inc VAT)													
(8) capital – Bill	7.0												
capital – family loan	5.0												
(9) sales	–	3.53	7.05	11.75	17.63	23.5	29.38	35.25	41.13	41.13	47.0	47.0	47.0
(10) VAT office				0.64									
Closing bank balance													
(11) projected borrowing	[4.54]	[8.7]	[19.59]	[26.69]	[28.57]	[30.44]	[40.33]	[36.73]	[32.02]	[39.7]	[30.55]	[23.23]	[29.7]

need are bought by the lessor (who may be a finance company) and then leased to you for an agreed rent. At the end of the contract it is usual for the leased equipment to be sold, and the greatest part of the proceeds (say 90 per cent) will then be returned to you as a rebate of rentals; or you may be able to continue leasing the equipment at a reduced rental.

The lessor claims any tax allowances (such as writing-down allowances) that may be available, and this is reflected in the level of the rental charges, which would otherwise be higher. You yourself can offset the whole rental against corporation tax.

The main advantage of leasing is that your working capital is not tied up in rapidly depreciating machinery and you can reduce your borrowing needs.

The first approach to the lessor generally has to come from you, the potential lessee (though some manufacturers, e.g. of office equipment, practise 'sales aid leasing' – the salesman approaches you fully prepared to arrange a lease). If you are new to the lessor, you may be required to establish your creditworthiness, for example, by providing a bank reference, but usually no security other than the leased goods is required; you may be asked to pay a few months' rental in advance. You have to specify exactly what equipment you want and, if the deal is approved, the lessor buys it from the manufacturer and leases it to you on the agreed terms.

Cars and some equipment (generally office or computer equipment) are leased for short periods and can sometimes be exchanged later for more up-to-date models. You should always try to deal with a lessor who will undertake to be responsible for maintaining the equipment; otherwise, you must be prepared to arrange your own maintenance contract.

Many major providers of lease finance to industry and commerce in the UK are members of the Equipment Leasing and Finance House Association. The Association's address is 18 Upper Grosvenor Street, London W1X 9PB · TEL 071-491 2783. You can ask for a booklet, *Equipment Leasing*, and a list of leasing companies to be sent to you. Most of them are London-based but operate in any part of the country. The Association also produces an annual report which gives an overview of the types of leasing business undertaken by members.

Hire-purchase is another way of obtaining plant and equipment without capital outlay. Just as in domestic purchases, you pay a deposit and then regular fixed instalments, and at the end of the contract the goods become your property. The instalment payments are generally higher than interest on a bank loan, but you may not wish to, or be able to, increase your bank loan, and the counterbalancing advantage is that in a hire-purchase agreement the terms are normally fixed, so that the charges cannot be increased if interest rates generally should rise.

Looking at the figures

Bill's case has several vital lessons for the new entrepreneur. First of all, you will certainly be surprised when you discover just how much money you are going to need as working capital. It is easy to underestimate one's requirements. Many businesses which are expanding make that mistake: they run out of money because they expand too rapidly. This is called overtrading.

Secondly, an estimated profit margin may appear ample, yet if the volume of sales turns out to be lower than the forecast, the total profits may fail to cover outgoings.

Nearly every first attempt at a profit and loss forecast is too ambitious. That is why a cash flow forecast is needed: to warn the small businessman or businesswoman when resources are not equal to ambitions.

It is easy to recast figures at the planning stage in order to deploy one's resources to best advantage, and arrive at a satisfactory and realistic forecast which can confidently be put before a bank or other financial organisation. However, it is terribly easy, when you have produced a forecast you do not like, to adjust the assumptions and figures – in that order – so that it all looks workable. You must look at original assumptions and new ones and see if you are not introducing too much wishful thinking.

Why you will need an accountant

If you already know something about business accounting and revel in figures, you may think that you can do without an accountant.

Bear in mind, though, that however nimble with numbers you may be, you are unlikely to have an accountant's grasp of the innumerable regulations relating to taxation or the relevant aspects of company and revenue law, nor his or her experience in dealing with the Board of Inland Revenue, nor the all-round familiarity with different aspects of business. Here are some of the problems with which an accountant can help you:

- to decide whether to set up as a sole trader, partnership or a limited company
- to find ways of raising capital
- to set up cash flow forecasts and profit and loss forecasts
- to decide whether to register for VAT if you do not have to
- to choose a starting date, and more important still, a trading year end date
- to keep day-to-day records, account books and ledgers
- to claim all possible allowances and reliefs against tax, and to negotiate with the tax inspector
- to claim expenses
- to cope with pensions, annuities and insurance.

Choosing an accountant must be done carefully. It is necessary to make sure that someone has proper qualifications (look for the letters FCA or ACA after someone's name). Use the *Yellow Pages* to find names and addresses. If you want a full list of chartered accountants practising in your area, contact your local District Society of Chartered Accountants.

For more information contact the Institute of Chartered Accountants. It publishes several useful booklets, including *Setting Up in Business, Choosing a Chartered Accountant* and *Why You Need a Chartered Accountant*. These and further details can be obtained from The Institute of Chartered Accountants in England & Wales, PO Box 433, Moorgate Place, London EC2P 2BJ.

CHAPTER **3**

HOW ARE YOU GOING TO TRADE?

YOU WILL have to decide whether to trade as a sole trader, in a partnership, or as a limited company. A co-operative is a much less usual business form, but may also be worth considering. You can usually change to another legal entity later, as your business develops.

Deciding how to trade should be an integral part of your plans, and is something that you should discuss with your professional adviser. There are various considerations, and some which might be significant for your business could be quite unimportant for another.

As to considerations of taxation, what you must do is compare the trading position of a sole trader or partnership and that of a company; and also compare your own position as a sole trader or partner, with your position as a shareholder-owner and salaried director of a limited company. You have to decide what aspects of taxation are most important for you.

For instance, you are obviously not going into business to lose money, but some businesses are likely, in their early years, to make losses which are useful for tax purposes. If you are trading as a company, these losses are carried forward and set against profits in future years. If you are a sole trader (or partnership), you can do this too, but there is also scope for carrying the losses sideways, and setting them against any other income you may receive, and scope for carrying them back to earlier years.

The choice may not be clear-cut, but you should try to assess where the balance of advantage lies. Circumstances may change, so you should periodically review your choice. It is usually possible to change from sole trader (or partnership) to a company without too many tax snags: changing the other way is more difficult.

Sole trader

Being a sole trader does not mean you have to work alone, but that you are totally and solely responsible for the business. You take all the profits, but you are also personally liable for all the debts incurred to the full extent of your means. Should you not have the money in the business to pay your business debts, your personal possessions, including your home, could be taken in settlement.

Many small businesses start as sole traders and are later turned into limited companies.

Partnership

A business partnership is an association of two or more people (up to 20) trading together as one firm and sharing the profits. A single tax assessment is made on the profits of a partnership, so that what is shared out represents post-tax profits. And if one partner should abscond, the others have to pay all the outstanding tax, including what would have been the absconder's share. In cases of losses, all the partners can be held liable for the whole of the firm's debts, to the full extent of their personal means, just as though they were a sole trader.

It is wise, in a partnership, to have a simple agreement, drawn up by a solicitor and setting out each partner's share of the profits, and how each partner's share is to be valued if he or she wants to withdraw from the partnership, or a new partner comes in; and, if one of the partners dies, what should happen to his or her share.

The agreement should state for how long the partnership is to run or under what conditions it can be terminated. Partnerships that go sour can be messy and upsetting, so it is wise to lay down guidelines of who does what and what should happen in the case of a dispute. Other points that must be agreed are: how much can each partner draw (e.g. monthly) on account of his or her share of the profit? Are there equal voting rights? Who signs the cheques?

What are the arrangements for holidays, and what happens in the case of long illness? What happens if an ex-partner wants to start trading in competition?

All the partners may work in the firm; or one or more of them may be 'sleeping partners' who just put in money. A partnership agreement can include any clauses specific to the particular set of circumstances.

Sole traders and partnerships may trade under their own name or names, or else under another name or title. However, if the name that you have chosen to trade under is not your own surname(s), you must indicate the name(s) of the owner(s) on all stationery, and display them in your shop or office or place of work.

Limited company

A limited company is a legal entity, just as though it were a person, and must be conducted according to rules laid down by company law. They include the maintenance of accounts, an annual audit, and the disclosure of the company's activities to the general public.

The shareholder/s (there need only be one) are the owners of the company, but are liable for its debts only to the extent of the face value of their shares. However, a director's liability can be extended by personal guarantees that he or she may have given to a bank or other financial institution as security for a business loan. Under the 1986 Insolvency Act, directors are made personally liable and subject to criminal prosecution if they continue trading or take credit knowing that the company is insolvent.

Limited companies may be public or private. If public ('plc'), the shares may be made available to the general public and may be quoted on the Stock Exchange. Private companies – the majority – do not offer shares to the public, and style themselves 'Limited' or 'Ltd'.

Formalities

The following addresses are where limited companies must be registered.

- Registrar of Companies, Companies House, Crown Way, Maindy, Cardiff CF4 3UZ   TEL (0222) 388588 (in England and Wales)
- Registrar of Companies, Companies House, 100–102 George Street, Edinburgh EH2 3DJ   TEL 031-225 5774 (in Scotland)
- Companies Registry, IDB House, 64 Chichester Street, Belfast BT1 4JX   TEL (0232) 234488 (in Northern Ireland).

Registration entails submitting a memorandum of association which must include details of the name of the company, its country of registration, the objects of the company, statement of the limited liability of its members, the amount of share capital and how it is divided into shares. It must be properly signed and witnessed.

You may also submit articles of association (which is something different from the memorandum). They cover a variety of internal matters: broadly speaking, they deal with the rights and powers of the directors and the members; meetings; votes; issue of new shares and restrictions on transfer of shares, such as the right of first refusal for the other members if one of them wishes to dispose of his shares. It is very often easiest simply to say that the standard articles under the Companies Act will apply, and then to list such alterations and additions to them as suit one's particular circumstances.

There are other necessary forms on registration: details of (and consent to act by) first directors and secretary; precise address of the company's registered office; and a statutory declaration that all the formalities have been complied with.

The fees payable on registration are as follows: £50 for a new incorporation; £50 for a change of company name; £32 a year thereafter, for filing the company's annual return with the Registrar of Companies. A same-day service for registration or change of company name is available: current fees are £200 for registration; £200 for a change of name or re-registration.

It is important to have professional help in registering a company. Some lawyers and accountants specialise in this.

Also, there are company registration agents, through whom you can 'buy' a company off the shelf. The agent has registered the company with stand-in directors, shareholders and secretary, but the company is not operating. When you buy the company, your names are substituted for those of the stand-ins.

If you buy a ready-made company set-up, its name may not be to your liking, but you can change this through Companies House.

Your choice of trading name must conform to the rules laid down by the Companies Act 1985 and the Business Names Act 1985 (in Northern Ireland, the Business Names (Northern Ireland) Order 1986) which are designed to enable anyone dealing with a business to know the owner's name and address. They amount, briefly, to this: the owner of a business must disclose his or her surname (if it is a sole trader) or surnames (if it is a partnership) or full corporate name (if it is a limited company), together with the address in each case, on the business premises and stationery, if he or she chooses to trade under some name other than the surname(s) or corporate name. So, for example, if you trade as R. Random; or (Roderick) Random and (Humphrey) Clinker; or Peregrine Pickles Ltd., you are not affected, but formulations such as 'Random's Travel Agency', or 'The Perfect Pickle' will require compliance with the disclosure rules. A complete explanation of these and other rules relating to business names is available in *Notes for Guidance on Business Names and Business Ownership* from the Registrar of Companies.

Co-operative

A co-operative is a business enterprise which is jointly owned by its members. A *worker co-operative* is owned and controlled by its employees; a *consumer co-operative* by its customers; a *community co-operative* by the community which the co-operative serves; a *service* or *secondary co-operative* by the users of the services provided (such as a group of small businesses collectively owning and managing their premises).

A co-operative may be a co-ownership, with the workers owning shares in the equity of the business in proportion to their investment in it; or it may be a common ownership, with the assets being collectively owned.

A co-operative may be registered under the Industrial and Provident Societies Acts, with members having limited liability, or it may be incorporated as a limited company. An I&PS co-operative must always have at least seven members, not all of whom need be workers in the business; a limited-company co-operative needs only two members.

Most new co-operatives register either as an I&PS (Industrial and Provident Society) or as a company limited by guarantee, using one of the sets of model rules available from ICOM (Industrial Common Ownership Movement), or SCDC (Scottish Co-operative Development Committee Ltd). Model rules make registration easier, cheaper and quicker than having a constitution drawn up, but ICOM and SCDC provide a 'tailor-made' service on request. SCDC also has model rules for companies limited by shares which can participate in the Business Expansion Scheme. Costs vary between the different agencies and the different legal structures.

The registration process takes about six to eight weeks – much longer if any queries should arise. Adopting the model rules, which are already accepted by the Registrar, helps to prevent this.

The essence of a co-operative is that it is run for the benefit of its members and has a democratic constitution: everyone who qualifies may become a member and has one vote, irrespective of the size of his or her investment. This does not mean that every issue is put to the vote: while very small co-operatives may involve all the members in day-to-day management matters, most of the 1,500 registered co-operatives delegate these powers to an elected committee, which remains accountable to the membership. Few worker co-operatives employ a paid manager in the conventional sense of the word, but it is common in the other types.

A co-operative must, of course, be commercially viable if it is to survive and compete with other enterprises, and must be conducted on proper business lines. However, when profits are generated, any surplus is generally distributed amongst members in proportion to the extent to which they have traded with or taken part in the business of the society. And though a co-operative may not need to produce a dividend, it must still be able to meet its interest payments and capital repayments on loans.

The principle of co-operation may help to keep the enterprise afloat where ordinary companies would founder. For instance, during difficult trading times members may be willing to reduce their expectations and even make some sacrifices for the good of the whole organisation.

Co-operatives may start in different ways. Most are new-start businesses, but some are formed by workers or members of the community to take over existing businesses, including ones which have failed in the hands of conventional management. This option, the so-called 'phoenix' co-operative, is by no means simple, and though the attempt may attract much publicity, in most cases it will be possible only if the original business is scaled down considerably before being revived as a co-operative.

New-start co-operatives are created by groups of individuals who wish to combine their skills or pursue a common interest to create a democratically controlled business; or by members of a community (which may be a geographical community or a 'community of interest') who create a co-operative to provide themselves with a service that they need; or by small businesses which wish to own and manage collectively resources needed by all, such as premises or marketing.

If you are considering establishing your business as a co-operative, you will need specialist advice. Most areas of the country are served by either a local Co-operative Development Agency, or by local authority officers with specific responsibility for co-operatives. If neither of these facilities is available to you, or you do not know how to contact them, ICOM will be able to advise you.

Getting help

Among the places to go for help or information are:

Industrial Common Ownership Movement (ICOM)
ICOM promotes and advises worker co-operatives and other forms of employee ownership; provides specialist registration and legal services for co-operatives and community enterprises; offers training and consultancy services; has an extensive mail-order catalogue of publications; can assist in raising money from Europe for co-operative training schemes; and provides legal, technical and practical services to its members. Membership is

open to all co-operatives, support organisations and sympathisers.

Industrial Common Ownership Movement, Vassalli House, 20 Central Road, Leeds LS1 6DE   TEL (0532) 461737.

Industrial Common Ownership Finance Limited (ICOF)
ICOF administers a revolving loan fund on a national basis for co-operative enterprises. It has specific loan funds for particular areas of the country.

Typical loans are for £10,000 over five years at 12½ per cent interest. Enterprises which apply for such loans must be able to demonstrate their co-operative status, and also their commercial viability.

Industrial Common Ownership Finance Limited (ICOF), 12–14 Gold Street, Northampton NN1 1RS   TEL (0604) 37563.

Registry of Friendly Societies
The society gives information and advice about rules and registration.

Register of Friendly Societies, 15 Great Marlborough Street, London W1V 2AX   TEL 071-437 9992.

The Scottish Co-operatives Development Company Ltd
This organisation offers guidance to groups of people wishing to form a workers' co-operative. Such advice covers all forms of business consultancy and there is now a venture capital company available to provide capital requirements for new and existing co-operatives in the whole of Scotland.

The Scottish Co-operatives Development Company Ltd, Templeton Business Centre, Templeton Street, Bridgeton, Glasgow G40 1DA   TEL 041-554 3797.

Management buy-outs

A lot of publicity has been given in recent years to employees buying the business in which they work. This is, in fact, an opportunity which arises only rarely; the owner's motives for selling the business (and, of course, the accounts of the business) should be scrutinised very carefully.

Unless you know exactly why the original company went out of business, and have definite proposals for putting things right, you will not find it easy to raise the necessary finance.

If you have been made redundant by the winding up of a company, consider whether there is any part of the operation or assets (some of the workshop plant, for instance) that you could buy and use in starting a project of your own. If a company has been wound up and its workforce made redundant, there may be equipment available for purchase, perhaps even part of the company's operation.

There is little to stop employees who leave an existing company from setting up in competition. Even if there is a clause in their contract of employment restricting their future business ventures, the courts will not uphold a contract that is a restraint of trade and denies anyone the right to earn a living. However, the ex-employer may stop former employees from making use of his or her trade secrets or confidential information by taking out an injunction.

Always be cautious, and make sure you do not overcommit yourself financially.

Franchises

The principle involved in franchising is basically this: a company which is successful in manufacturing a product or providing a service decides to extend its activities nationally or internationally. Instead of setting up its own company-owned branches, it becomes a *franchisor*, selling its experience and established reputation to individuals, the *franchisees*.

Franchises – a ready-made business identity

The purchase of a franchise is the purchase of the right to use a particular method to run a particular kind of business. You are buying expertise and an image, sometimes the right to use and trade under a household name. The entry price can be considerable – it is for you to assess whether the potential rewards are commensurate.

Becoming a franchisee usually means that you will own the business assets (premises, equipment and so on) – although some franchisors prefer to own the business premises and lease them to franchisees. But you will certainly not own the business method. You will be at liberty to decide the most appropriate method of trading, whether as sole trader, in a partnership or through a limited company.

A vast array of 300 or more franchises can be purchased. These range from the fast food industry (Wimpy, Kentucky Fried Chicken) to service industries (Prontaprint, Dynarod). In acquiring a franchise, you are able to appear to the public to be something that you are not, namely the outpost of a considerable business empire.

You will not however be allowed to impress your own personal stamp on the image of the business. Your business operation, and your trading accounts in particular, will be subject to scrutiny by a (it is to be hoped, reasonably benevolent) Big Brother.

You must be very clear from the outset about one point: you will be buying a right to trade for a limited period only, typically five years. This may be coupled with the right to renew the franchise at the end of that period. The cost to you will be the payment of a capital sum on entering into the agreement, and probably also further sums (service fees) during its currency. These latter may be related to sales or turnover, or both.

While you will need to vet thoroughly any prospective franchisor, you must expect also to be vetted by it; indeed, the better the organisation you are thinking of joining, the more concerned it is likely to be to wish to ensure that only franchisees of high calibre are taken on. So you will each need to make a good impression on the other.

The clearing banks have specialised departments that deal with, and advise on, franchises. Understandably they take the view that the purchase of a suitable franchise helps to minimise the risks of starting up a business. You will, of course, need to make your own capital contribution to the initial costs; a bank will generally expect this to be at least 30 per cent of the total. Subject to this point, the raising of capital will be likely to be more straightforward than in starting a business from scratch.

How does the franchising system work?

There are no hard and fast rules, because the diversity of businesses and business ideas inevitably gives rise to very different systems.

At the core of the agreement will be an operations manual incorporating the essential business techniques which you, as franchisee, are obliged to use. Expect a franchisor to stipulate exactly what accounting systems you are to use (he or she will need uniformity among franchisees since he or she will be inspecting their accounts and may want to draw management information from them); how you are required to run the business. Opening hours may be stipulated; in the case of a shop, the franchisor may retain complete control over the décor and furnishings and training of staff. The particular methods and techniques of, for example, preparing and cooking the food (in a fast food chain) may be laid down – you may, in this case, be obliged to buy certain foodstuffs and ingredients only from the franchisor. The operations manual is, of course, a confidential document and its contents, trade secrets and knowhow must not be revealed.

You will be required by the franchisor to enter into a contract (a franchise agreement). You should take professional advice on this and will need to understand how it deals with issues such as:

- The initial training to be provided by the franchisor. This should provide you with the requisite skills to run the business efficiently. This is part of what you are buying with your initial capital sum.
- The level of back-up which the franchisor is obliged to provide, such as advertising and general promotion, advice and troubleshooting. This is, in effect, the return which you get for the service fees charged. The franchisor is entitled to a profit. Similarly, you are entitled to an efficient back-up service from him or her and ought to know that there is an obligation to spend money for the good of the network of franchisees and to continue to take an interest in it.
- What goods and provisions you are obliged to buy through the franchisor, and what controls there are over the price which he or she charges for them.

- Whether you have exclusive trading rights as franchisee in a defined geographical area. This is generally regarded as one of the key elements of a franchise.
- How long the franchise runs, and on what terms it is renewable.
- Whether any restrictions on trading will affect you when the franchise comes to an end.
- Whether the continuation of the franchise is dependent on a minimum level of turnover or profit or any other factors. (When you have parted with what may have been a sizeable capital sum, it would be disastrous if the franchise could be withdrawn unfairly.)
- What will happen if you want (or are obliged) to sell the business. The better franchisors are likely to insist on complete control over the vetting of any new franchisee, so your ability to sell as a going concern may be dependent on the franchisor's goodwill and/or the quality of the prospective buyer. The potential problem here is that of being left with only the shell of a business to sell, but no goodwill. One solution would be to insist that the franchisor is obliged to purchase the business from you if no other satisfactory franchisee can be found to step into your shoes.

However, most franchisors use standard forms of franchise agreement and are not prepared to allow significant changes to them. The justification offered is the need for uniformity in business operations.

Some words of warning

For a franchise to be successful, it needs to combine a successful business idea with a proper level of support and promotion from the franchisor. If a capital sum is payable for an exclusive right to distribute goods or offer a certain service within a given area, but no back-up is offered, think hard whether you could set up a similar operation yourself and perhaps save a great deal of money.

Cowboy franchisors also exist. They charge a relatively high buy-in fee but offer little or no training or equipment. Or the sum involved may be low – about £5,000, say, which is modest by ethical franchising standards – but when you look into what you would be getting for this, you may realise that there is very little tangible return.

The most tell-tale sign of a franchisor who is not above-board is that he demands an excessively high franchise fee and management service fee. Ten per cent of turnover is average, though some franchisors may set a somewhat higher rate, in return for providing special facilities for franchisees; but anything grossly in excess of this should be regarded with suspicion.

Unscrupulous cowboy franchisors are happy to take your money for what at first sight seems a sound business idea, but if you do not end up with a distinctive product or service to offer, you should probably leave well alone. In any event, be sure to have any potential franchise agreement thoroughly vetted by your solicitor, and the financial side of the undertaking by your accountant. You will need to establish:

- Whether the franchisor is a member of the British Franchise Association (see below). A member is bound by a code of ethics designed to protect franchisees.
- What experiences other franchisees have had. A reputable franchisor cannot have grounds to refuse a request for a list of its franchisees.

Finally, ask yourself this question: if the business idea is such a money-spinner, why is the franchisor not running the business himself or herself – or is it the sale of the franchise that is the true money spinner?

A good business idea or method can warrant a substantial capital sum. But in taking on a franchise you will become a partner – but probably only a second-class one – in a business, and certainly the partner undertaking financial risk. You must decide whether the degree of outside control warrants the extra financial commitment.

It is best to deal with a franchisor who is a member of the British Franchise Association. The BFA has published a Franchisee Information Pack (£17.50 including postage and packing), available from Franchise Chambers, Thames View, Newtown Road, Henley-on-Thames, Oxfordshire RG9 1HG   TEL (0491) 578049.

Buying an existing business

The purchase of an existing business is usually undertaken by people who are already in business and wish to expand their operations or change business venues. But it makes equally sound economic sense for someone starting in business to acquire an established niche in a market. The main impediment is likely to be the cost.

The extra items for which you will have to pay on acquiring an established business are:

Stock
When starting a business from scratch, you have time in which to build up your customer base, and your stock level at inception will probably be a moderate one. By contrast, the value of the stock of some types of existing business may exceed the aggregate cost of the premises and goodwill.

Trade fittings
Business premises need furniture and other items of equipment and fittings – in a shop, these will include shelving, cash tills and perhaps freezers, etc, all of which must be bought from the seller.

Goodwill
A flourishing business is worth more than the sum of its constituent parts. The difference between the two is called goodwill, the value of which is affected principally by the turnover of the business. This is an oversimplification, since the value of the business is also affected by the figures attributed to items such as leases and fittings for the purposes of accounting and tax.

Goodwill – the indispensable aspect of business

The term 'goodwill' is used here as a general designation to cover customer loyalty and all other intangible (mainly external) factors which give a business its status and enable it to run profitably. It means different things in different businesses.

As a prospective buyer of an established business, you will need to satisfy yourself as far as possible either

- that the goodwill exists and will continue in existence after you take it over or;
- if the business is very run down and you are in reality taking over little more than a shell, that the goodwill will come into being when you run the business.

This is a tall order. Some of the factors which make the difference between success and failure are intangible, and are much more likely to be perceived by someone with previous business experience. But a commonsense approach and a sceptical stance will take you a long way to understanding the essentials of a business. Professional advice from an accountant and a solicitor experienced in business should not be dispensed with. Their investigations should bring to light any serious problems affecting the business.

An accountant's job is to scrutinise the business accounts. These will rarely tell the whole truth. However, they ought to contain sufficient of the truth to tell him or her how the business is structured financially, and from this your accountant will be able to calculate your financial requirements and to let you know whether you stand a chance of making a go of it. For example, a business from which the proprietor makes a comfortable living but on which there are no outstanding bank loans may be a potentially lethal trap for the buyer who needs to borrow heavily. The two proprietors have entirely different financial requirements. An experienced accountant should also be able to judge, from knowledge of other similar businesses, whether the accounts suggest that the business which you wish to buy differs in any important way from other such businesses. Unfortunately, there is no safeguard against an unscrupulous seller who falsifies his or her accounts, other than perhaps your instinct and that of the people advising and helping you.

A solicitor will advise you on the purchase contract, and the initial enquiries may bring in important information.

Local authority search and enquiries

These do not tell as much about a property and its locality as people generally suppose. Apart from road proposals affecting land within 200 metres of the property, a local authority search will only give information about the property itself: the effect of planning legislation, compulsory purchase or demolition orders, liability for road works, financial orders and other matters which could affect it. But the search will not provide information about other property.

So, if the next-door property is due to be demolished to make way for a hypermarket, you and your solicitor will be none the wiser from reading the result of a local search. If you want to know about current planning policy for the neighbourhood, you are entitled to inspect the planning register at the local authority offices. There you can read the planning history of all properties in the neighbourhood and also see what applications have been lodged but not yet decided on. You can also talk to the planning officials who will normally be glad to help and will tell you about local trends and developments. Look out for pointers to help you assess the future prospects of a business, such as:

- new housing in the neighbourhood – will this bring potential new customers?
- the diversion of a road, or the construction of a bypass – will this adversely affect passing trade or your accessibility to your customers?
- creation of a pedestrian precinct (which tends to boost trade for shops within the precinct) – might it perhaps draw trade away from businesses outside it?

Remember that planning permission is required for a property to be used for business purposes. You need to check (with your solicitor's help if necessary) that the premises have got the appropriate planning permission. If you think the nature of your business might change, this could call for a planning application – for example, to change from a grocer's shop to a snack bar.

Enquiries of the seller's solicitor

You will probably have made extensive enquiries of the seller about the business, to which many reassuring replies will have been given. But the seller is trying to persuade you to buy the business; he or she is not going to go out of the way to alert you to any problems. Inevitably, if there are problem areas, he or she is likely to want to paper over the cracks, and in doing so may give you information which is either misleading or untruthful. If you proceed to purchase on the basis of incorrect information (to use a neutral term), you may have some form of redress against the seller. However, recollection of what is said can be notoriously inaccurate; moreover, you will have the problem of proving what was said, and the only thing you can rely on is the seller denying what you claim he or she said.

There is a simple solution. Make sure that important questions are raised in writing by your solicitor and that satisfactory replies are given. An experienced solicitor should know the general queries which need to be raised, but it is for you to make sure that he or she also raises the points of particular concern to you, to cover areas such as:

- employees of the business (you need a lot of information about them in order to establish what redundancy and other rights they have)
- items on lease hire or hire-purchase: the seller cannot sell you items which do not legally belong to him or her, but you may want to take over the agreements
- any work carried out or changes of use for which planning permission would have been required
- compliance with fire precautions and other safety legislation
- the identity of the landlord (if the premises are leasehold) and method of paying rent, also whether there are or have been any disputes with the landlord
- what continuing contracts can be taken over by a purchaser
- protection of goodwill.

Is there more to it?

All these enquiries will not necessarily answer the most important question: will the business be a success for you? You need to investigate further. It helps if you can find out exactly why the business is being sold. The reason may be harmless, but there is a chance that the seller knows that the business is under some sort of threat, and is getting out while the going is good. Standard answers from sellers include retirement, poor health, moving out of the area or to a different type of business.

You will be taking over pending contracts, so check whether the seller has performed them satisfactorily so far, and whether you will be able to complete them properly, and on time.

If the business is a disaster for the seller, you will not be told directly that this is the case. But it may be revealed by the accounts.

Having satisfied yourself (so far as possible) that the business is viable, you should then try to analyse what makes it tick and to identify its strengths and any potential areas of weakness. Some businesses are heavily dependent on the personality of their owners and the departure of a popular owner from behind the counter may be followed by a decline in trade. Ask yourself also whether particular employees are vital to the image and success of the business. Some employees may be inclined to resign on the departure of a long-known boss, so you will have to win and make sure of the loyalty of any employees you regard as essential.

Last, but by no means least, take a long hard look at yourself. If the purchase proceeds, you will be one of the most important ingredients of the business. What makes you so special? (Answer this question honestly.)

The purchase – what is involved?

If the purchase of a business does not involve business premises, the transaction can be a very straightforward one. Nevertheless, you may be safer employing a solicitor. The most damaging thing that could happen is that the seller, having taken your money, immediately starts up in competition with you and wins back his or her old customers. Steps can be taken to protect you before the purchase is completed by ensuring that the seller enters into a non-competition covenant. Ask the solicitor to obtain the necessary covenant from the seller.

The majority of business purchases involve the purchase of business premises, freehold or leasehold. The position with regard to planning permission for the business must be thoroughly checked, as well as compliance with other relevant legislation. In addition, your solicitor should check whether there are any covenants adversely affecting the property or your ability to carry on a particular type of business from the premises, or whether the landlord's permission (in addition to planning permission) is required under the covenants for building work or change of use.

It is possible that with freehold covenants which were originally imposed many years ago, there is nobody legally entitled to enforce them; on the other hand, there could well be someone waiting to pounce if there is any infringement. It is possible to take out insurance for possible legal action for breach of covenants where investigation suggests that they are unenforceable.

There is a major difference between freehold and leasehold covenants. With the latter, there is inevitably someone – the landlord – who will check that they are being complied with and who will be able to take effective action if they are not.

Buying a lease?

Many business premises are leasehold, and certainly the great majority of premises found in high streets and shopping centres are so. (The simple reason is cost: freehold premises are financially beyond the reach of many people who are already in business and generally all the more so of people starting their own business or seeking to buy someone else's.)

In buying a lease, you are buying the right to occupy premises for a definite period of time. At the end of that period you are at liberty to quit the premises and hand them back to the landlord, but you also have the right to apply for a new lease. You should also have the right to sell the lease at any time you wish, but some leases prohibit this.

In buying leasehold premises you will almost certainly be buying the assignment of an existing lease that was negotiated between the landlord and the original tenant. This document will regulate your legal relationship with the landlord, so read it very carefully and get your solicitor to explain the more technical aspects of it.

A new lease is only likely to be negotiated if it is the landlord (the freeholder) who is the seller of the business. Inevitably, a landlord will seek to bias the document in his or her own favour, but there may be room for bargaining. Remember that it is worth taking the trouble to get the terms of the lease right – once it is agreed and signed, it must be assumed to be unchangeable.

A lease tends to be an intimidating document. But sit down and read it, and also the various schedules attached, and mark (in pencil and on a copy) the points which are important to you or which you do not understand. Ask for clarification and then read it again. Here is a brief guide to some of the issues with which the lease deals, and the questions you need to ask about it.

Rent
The rent will probably be payable in instalments each year. What is the current rent? When is it next due to be reviewed? Will the new rent be linked to the retail prices index (unlikely), or determined by reference to rentals of comparable premises? What other payments will be due to the landlord (for example, insurance, service charges)?

Length of lease
When does the lease come to an end? Are there any likely hindrances to a renewal? Does the landlord have the right to end it before it runs out?

Insurance
Who is responsible for what and how much are the premiums?

Permitted use
Is it adequate for your present and future business use? Can the landlord be required to consent to a change in permitted use? Is the marketability of the lease likely to be restricted when you want to sell it?

Repairs
Whose responsibility are they? To what standard? (Unless the landlord is fully responsible for repairs and the cost of repairs, make sure that you have a full structural survey of the premises carried out before you buy. Money spent on repairing someone else's property is money you will not see again.)

The premises
The description is important, if only to establish the limits of liability for repairs. Do they include the foundations? The roof? The loadbearing walls?

Subletting
Is it prohibited by the lease, or are any restrictions imposed?

Selling
The landlord will want to vet any prospective buyer (known as 'assignee'), but must approve unless he or she has good reason not to. In the deed which incorporates his or her permission for the sale (the 'licence to assign') the buyer is usually required to enter into covenants with the landlord. Some leases call for directors' guarantees where the buyer is a limited company.

Alterations
What kind of alterations can be carried out without permission from the landlord? Does the landlord's permission have to be obtained for business signs?

A lease deals with other important issues in addition to these. Knowing and understanding what it says will help you avoid problems – many disputes between landlord and tenant arise because one or the other of them did not take the trouble to consult the lease before taking action.

The purchase contract

The contract is the document which lays down the ground rules of the purchase. Before exchange of contracts between buyer and seller, either party is at liberty to withdraw from the transaction without being liable to reimburse the other's financial outlays. After exchange of contracts, both parties are legally committed to the transaction. Any attempt by either one to withdraw risks becoming a costly experience. In any event, avoid signing any document other than the contract (and any related legal documents) provided by your solicitor.

The contract usually stipulates how the purchase price is to be split between:

- the premises
- the business goodwill
- any business equipment being sold.

Make sure you take your accountant's advice on this, because it will almost certainly have important implications for both your income tax on starting in business and for your capital gains position if/when you eventually sell.

The contract will state what business stock (also known as stock in trade) is to be sold and on what basis it is to be valued. Valuations are carried out by buyer and seller, or by a professional stock valuer. The basis of valuation should be wholesale value, often determined by reference to its purchase price. Whether or not you are likely to have any use for all the stock once you are running the business, you must expect to have to buy it all. Its value cannot be accurately assessed until it is valued at completion, so make sure that you will have sufficient funds available even if the figure turns out to be a high one. You may be able to persuade the seller to guarantee that the stock will not exceed a certain level, but be careful – if you do not have sufficient stock when you start trading, you will at once be in difficulty.

The contract will also define the trade fittings and equipment sold with the business, often in a 'schedule annexed' (that just means a list). Check that the equipment is well maintained, in good order, with an acceptable working life before it. Some items will not actually belong to the seller. Business vehicles and cash registers are generally subject to hire-purchase agreements; display freezers are sometimes lent to shop owners; burglar alarm and telephone equipment is often leased on medium- to long-term contracts. The legal position with regard to such items will need to be clarified so that (where appropriate) any agreement with their owners can be transferred into the buyer's name (yours).

If you will need any form of licence (to sell alcohol, for example) or other special permission or approval to enable you to take over the business (for example, a rest home or nursing home), the contract may need to provide that the transaction will not be completed without it.

Goodwill and its protection

Goodwill is another important issue which should be dealt with in the contract. You are buying someone else's business but what essential elements of the business can be taken over, and how can you protect yourself against the seller taking your money and then setting up in competition?

It often happens that the name under which the seller trades is included in the sale. This provides a strong appearance of continuity, and will be important if you are taking over a flourishing business, but of no value if you intend to change the name (and thus probably the image) of the business. Some trading names warrant the registration of a service mark (see Chapter 11). But not all names are the seller's to sell. For example, to trade as a Unipart Centre, a buyer will have to be approved by Unipart (this is a limited form of franchising).

Any existing custom of the business should also be included in the definition of goodwill. However, it will be entirely up to the customers whether they wish to continue to patronise the business. But a buyer would be wise to obtain a covenant from the seller which prohibits the seller from soliciting the customers of the business, and perhaps also prohibits him or her from involvement in any competing business within a defined area for a defined period.

The precise terms in which such a covenant is phrased will depend on the type and location of the business that is being sold. With many businesses, the first few weeks or months of trading are going to determine the extent of customer loyalty, and a lengthy ban on competition from the seller will not be necessary.

After exchange of contracts

It may be prudent to check all the items of trade fittings and equipment against the schedule immediately before completion. You will also need to finalise arrangements with the seller for stocktaking – ensure that this is done after he or she has stopped trading and before you start doing so.

The format of the business

If the seller runs the business in the form of a limited company, he or she will have taken advice on the best way to sell it, and you may find that he or she wants to sell it in the same form: not as just a business, but as a company. He or she does that by selling all the issued shares in exchange for a single lump sum: you then become owner of the company, and have yourself appointed director in his or her place.

You may think that this is no different from buying a business in the form of a sole trader: but there is a difference, and it is not to your advantage. When you buy a business in the form of a sole trader, it then has a new and different owner (you), and any problems from past years – to do, for example, with taxation or money claim – will still be the seller's problems. You will probably be able to ignore them unless you choose to settle them, in order to enhance the business's goodwill and reputation.

But if you buy the business as a company, it still has the same owner – the company – and you inherit all past and many prospective problems, which could involve you in considerable expenditure of time and money, and prevent you from starting with a clean slate.

That is why the apparently simple matter of transferring shares is, in practice, supported by a long, complicated contract which contains, amongst other items, a great many warranties and indemnities in favour of the buyer. But if the seller is later found to have no money any more, these will not be worth anything.

It is wiser, therefore, to insist on buying the business without buying the company. This can be done in the name of your own company (if that is how you want to trade), and the seller should retain the original company.

If he or she refuses, you will have to decide whether to take the risk, or let the deal fall through.

Becoming a shareholder

The sale of shares in a limited company is a method frequently employed in order to raise finance, but its effect is of course to transfer part of the ownership of the company and (normally) a corresponding degree of control over it to the new owner, be they investor or otherwise.

If the owner of a limited company wants to take in a 'partner', he or she will do so by selling a portion of his or her shareholding. Care should be exercised if you are considering taking this route, although the previous owner's continuing involvement (financial and managerial) in the business will, with luck, help to safeguard the prosperity of the company.

If one of several shareholders in a private company is seeking to sell his or her shareholding, bear in mind that the approval of the sale by the company directors may be crucial – since they are likely to have the right to veto any sale by the simple expedient of refusing to register a transfer of shares.

The value of a company is relatively easy to determine, although there are differing accounting conventions for doing so. But the value of a partial shareholding – particularly a minority shareholding – in the same company can be very difficult both to assess and to realise. The most important variable factor will be any restrictions that may exist on the owner's ability to sell. If the other shareholders are the only available market, you may have either to accede to their price or else to hang on to your shares – a dilemma that arises all too frequently.

These problems can be circumvented by agreement between the shareholders, but it is important that you take sound legal advice before committing yourself.

Becoming a partner

Becoming a partner in an existing business is very different from becoming a member (shareholder) in an existing limited company. Your legal liabilities to the outside world only start from the moment you become a partner; by contrast, the purchase of company shares brings with it all the skeletons lurking in the company's cupboards. But if buying shares necessarily implies a stake in all the company's assets, entering into a partnership does not automatically mean that you will acquire any rights of ownership over the partnership assets.

It is important to enter into a written agreement with the existing partners covering at least such essential issues as profit sharing and ownership of the firm's assets. These issues may at first seem clear-cut, but on reflection you will find that they are not. In the long run, ambiguity and uncertainty, if unresolved, only lead to unnecessary conflict.

CHAPTER 4

Marketing and selling

MARKETING and selling your product or service are not just incidental to producing it: they are the lifeblood of the business.

The two terms are not interchangeable. Marketing covers everything from research, product planning and development to promotion and, of course, selling. Selling is the process of negotiating and carrying out that transaction.

Emerson was mistaken: the world will not beat a path to your house to clamour for your better mousetrap. However efficient it may be, if you do not go to town and seek out people with mice, it will be left on your hands.

In fact, before you started to design it, you should have checked on the mouse population, and the cat population too; it never does to ignore one's competitors.

What is more, when you have found your customers, and are busy with orders, you must plan for future sales. Selling is a continuous process: you should always be looking ahead and planning your marketing strategy for the coming months and years.

The time to start planning for sales is when your product or service is still on the drawing-board. At this point, nothing is lost if you discover that your idea, however good of its kind, will not command a large enough market to make a profit. Perhaps it will be so expensive to produce that its price will be prohibitive; or, perhaps, there are not enough people who long for, say, reproduction antique musical boxes. You still have a chance to rethink it and eliminate expensive labour-intensive processes, for example; or modify it to give it more popular appeal; or scrap it altogether in favour of something else.

Begin by asking yourself some questions:

- What exactly have I got to offer my customers?
- Who are likely to be my customers, and where shall I find them?
- Who are my competitors, and in what way is my product an improvement on theirs or a better alternative (mousetrap v. poison)?
- What is the best way of making my product or service known to the customer?
- When do I start planning for the future?

What exactly have I got to offer?

Defining just what it is that you are going to put on the market cannot be done in isolation. You will also have to consider to whom, how, when, and where you are going to sell.

Consider your product

If what you are going to sell is something produced by other people, for which you are going to act as retailer or middleman, agent or dealer, you probably have no influence on the actual form of the product. The choice is between one brand and another, between the cheap and popular or the expensive and exclusive varieties of the product.

However, if it is something you have produced or designed (or had designed for you) and intend to produce, you can decide what the final form of the product will be. You can decide to produce it in several versions, with varying functions and at different price levels; you may make it highly specialised, with only one use, or you may incorporate several functions, in order to widen its appeal; or make it part of a range of related products; or change the materials of which it is made; or scrap it altogether and start again. Do not fall in love with the original idea and insist on going through with it, come hell or high water.

It may be unwise to include every possible refinement right from the start; a highly specialised product may appeal only to a small market. A simpler version may sell better and also pave the way for a more complex one, to be developed now and introduced at a later stage, incorporating new features in response to what were the first customers' reactions.

If your product is more sophisticated than the prospective buyers are likely to demand, or too expensive for the ultimate consumer, you must simplify the product or decide to find another market for it, or produce two varieties for different types of user.

If the product requires the skills of several craftsmen, for example cabinet-maker and precision engineer, make sure from the start that you will have a supply of skilled labour to depend on. It is no use building up a market for a product if you cannot maintain the supply. It might be better to design something that can be made by less skilled labour.

Ask yourself if the demand for your product is likely to be seasonal. A new nutcracker, for example, however super-efficient, is likely to sell readily only in the period before Christmas, so you may need another product (or several) to keep your plant and labour occupied for the rest of the year.

Where what you have to sell is quite simply a service plus your expertise, the need to define it precisely applies just as much as to a product. If, for example, you are setting up a security business, you should decide whether you are best able to supply a delivery service (complete with armoured cars), or human guards, or guard dogs, or specialist advice on how people can improve the security of their home or factory.

In the case of a consultancy or agency, too, define your scope as closely as possible, and relate it to your own experience. Rather than grandly planning to become an import-export agent, aim to trade with particular geographical areas and in specific products, preferably areas and products with which you are already familiar. When setting up as a consultant, you are more likely to succeed if you closely limit your field to where your particular expertise lies. Do not wait for your clients' reactions to tell you on what topics you are not qualified to give advice.

Who are my customers and where shall I find them?

The nature of the product or service will dictate a general answer: woollen sweaters are for people, automated filing systems are for offices, easy-to-install damp-proof window frames should interest the building industry and the d-i-y enthusiast. A solar-panel water heating system may have limited use in Britain, but could be the basis of an export trade.

Next, get some notion of how you should sell your products to your prospective customers, whether through a retail shop or a department store, through a wholesaler or by mail order, through agents or directly, in the UK or abroad.

Some market research

Researching your market is not as formidable as it sounds. You can do a lot of 'market research' yourself from sources ready to hand, starting with public libraries.

The central library in your area should have a comprehensive reference department. In the commercial section you will find trade directories and publications relating to your business; *Yellow Pages* and phone books covering the whole country; directories of foreign importers; official digests of statistics, and much else.

In London, you can command the superb resources of the Central Reference Library's commercial and technical section, but the chief town or city in your area should offer facilities.

The Government Statistical Service makes available, on demand, a vast amount of information gathered by government departments, and by the Business Statistics Office and the Office of Population Censuses and Surveys. The booklet *Government Statistics: A Brief Guide to Sources*, available free from the Information Services Division, Press Office (CSO), Great George Street, London SW1P 3AQ   TEL 071-270 6363/4, lists the various kinds of facts and figures available, including aspects of business, such as industrial production; financial services; the retail trade; external trade. Much of this is published in a series called *Business Monitors*.

Someone planning a comprehensive marketing strategy may want to study figures relating to national income and expenditure and population trends and projections. This may sound grandiose but what it amounts to is that you might get an idea of what proportion of what kind of people (teenagers, pensioners, etc) is likely to want your product.

Some publications for useful facts and figures include: *Classified List of Manufacturing Businesses* (issued in 10 parts); *Quarterly Statistics of Manufacturers' Sales; Population Trends* (quarterly); *Family Expenditure Survey* (annual); *Overseas Trade Statistics of the United Kingdom* (monthly) and *Annual Statistics on Retail Traders*. It is better to ask for them at the public library as they are rather expensive.

Useful free publications, such as *Marketing; Exporting; Selling to Large Firms*, are available from the Small Firms Service. To find out the address of your nearest Small Firms Centre, from which you can get much valuable information, dial 100 and ask the operator for Freephone Enterprise.

Trade organisations, trade journals, trade exhibitions

As a novice, you should snatch at every opportunity of consulting those who are already experts: your own trade organisation should be able to help you. Trade associations are listed in the Directory of British Associations (available in reference libraries). Journals and exhibitions will inform you about the prospects of your trade, future developments and new products, and will give you an idea of whom some of your potential buyers might be. The *Financial Times* publishes the dates and venues of forthcoming trade exhibitions. So, too, does the *Exhibition Bulletin*, 266–272 Kirkdale, Sydenham, London SE26 4RZ TEL 081-778 2288. The information it offers is worldwide in scope and two years or more in advance, which makes planning ahead easier.

If your product is to be sold to some trade or industry, you can use its trade directories to compile a list of potential customers.

You may find details of some more relevant journals and publications by looking at Brads Media Lists which are categorised by subject.

Chambers of Commerce and Chambers of Trade, besides being a source of information, may allow you access to their libraries.

Wherever economics or business studies are taught, at universities, local technical colleges, schools of business studies, you should be able to find a library, experts to consult, even students willing, for a modest fee, to do your market research for you. Make the arrangement, preferably in the autumn term, through the Management Studies or Trading Department.

Dry run

If you have started to manufacture your product in your spare time and are wondering whether to go into full production, try to test your market. This can be done for a small outlay, perhaps by distributing a few hundred leaflets, or putting a couple of dozen cards in shop windows. Do not distribute too many leaflets at a time, in case you would then not be able to deal with the number of requests. Space out the distribution. This should give you some idea of whether anyone in the district is interested in what you have to offer.

Who are my competitors?

Yellow Pages will tell you what other similar businesses there are in your area, if you are counting on local trade.

Make yourself familiar with your competitors' products. Watch particularly for competitors' publicity and advertising: yours will have to be different and better. Send for their promotional literature and price lists, attend trade exhibitions. Trade directories and the trade press will give you relevant addresses.

If yours is a service industry, try approaching a similar firm for advice. You may find one operating in another area remarkably willing to show you round the premises and answer questions. But do not expect your local firms to welcome and train more competition, and do not, in your enthusiasm, give your ideas away to someone who may beat you to it.

If the competitor's product is sold through retail outlets, go and see it at the point of sale to find out how it is displayed and promoted.

The object is to find out how your product would compare. Has it any unique features? Why should people prefer it to any other? What special features have the other products got that could be incorporated in your product (with due regard to infringement of copyright or patents)? Something as simple as a hook, a lid, a heatproof base, could make all the difference to the appeal of a gadget.

How do I sell my products?

The actual business of putting anything on the market has several aspects including advertising, sales and distribution, and pricing.

Advertising and promotion

Which of the various media you should use will depend very much on the nature of your product (or service), and how much you can afford to spend on making it known.

The local press is particularly suited to a service or business which relies on local customers, such as a plumber, electrician, hairdresser, launderette, florist. The cheapest advertisement is an insert in the classified advertisement section. This kind of advertisement does not catch the eye: it simply waits for someone looking for that type of service or product. So, to be effective, it should appear regularly.

If you want to catch the reader's passing glance, a display advertisement will be more effective or, if your budget permits, a larger, specially designed advertisement, placed on an editorial page (perhaps with a coupon on which further information can be requested, but then the return postage must be budgeted for). Such an advertisement, too, should appear regularly. A coupon is most effective when placed on the outside edge of the page, where it is easy to cut out.

Many local papers undertake the design of a display advertisement but a professionally designed one is likely to be more eye-catching. You can find a graphic designer through *Yellow Pages*, but before commissioning him or her, make sure you know the cost.

Advertising in national newspapers and magazines is suited to a firm hoping to sell by mail order. It is essential to choose publications that are right for the type of goods – women's clothing in women's pages and magazines, sets of spanners in d-i-y magazines.

The trade press is the medium for goods that are sold not to individual consumers but to other firms. Much the same considerations apply as in the case of the national press; and where your advertisement is likely to appear cheek-by-jowl with those of competitors, it is essential to have an effective display that stands out. There are plenty of small local advertising agencies whose names can be found in *Yellow Pages* or obtained from the Institute of Practitioners in Advertising (IPA), 44 Belgrave Square, London SW1X 8QS   TEL 071-235 7020. Ask to see specimens of work and get an estimate before you engage one.

What you will be paying for is know-how. An agency should be able to design your advertising, advise on its content and wording, and place it in the appropriate media at the right times.

Trade exhibitions and local trade fairs have a triple function – for market research, for finding out what your competitors are producing, and also for selling your own goods to firms. They are not usually open to the general public. Your trade press will tell you where and when appropriate exhibitions are taking place, and where to apply to book space. There may be several suitable ones each year.

Exhibitions can be expensive; as well as hiring the stand, you must arrange for someone competent to be there to run it, explain and perhaps demonstrate your product, distribute literature and note down enquiries (to be scrupulously followed up). Probably that person will have to be you, with consequent loss of your valuable time. The exhibition should at least earn back its expenses eventually, so do not rush in too readily without thought and preparation.

You are more likely to attract the buyers' attention if you write to them beforehand, preferably by name (which you can find out by telephoning their firms). Send them your promotional literature and the number of your stand, and invite them to have a chat with you.

If you cannot afford a stand, or if your range of goods does not rate one, ask the Chamber of Commerce or your Small Business Club for the names of any other firms who might be willing to share a stand. Or you may be able to find out from the promoters of the exhibition the names of firms who are exhibiting related products. Approach them to ask if they will lease you a share of their space and attendants.

Direct mail advertising

With direct mail advertising, you approach the customer directly, and by name. You send out a sales letter, accompanied by a leaflet, brochure or catalogue. The promotional literature should be eye-catching, designed by a professional, if possible.

Making the most of the post

Business Reply and Freepost are two of the services offered by the Royal Mail to direct mail advertisers. With Business Reply, you send out, for your customer's reply, a postcard or envelope printed with your address and needing no stamp: first and second class options are available. With Freepost, the customer can use either pre-printed cards or envelopes provided by you (first or second class), or use his or her own stationery (second class only). No stamp is needed if the word 'Freepost' is added to the address.

You pay only the postage, first or second class as you wish, plus a small handling charge on each reply you receive, in addition to an annual licence fee.

A prepayment is required, equivalent to an estimated one month's charges. If this proves an under- or over-estimate, the charges for the following months are adjusted accordingly.

If you want to direct your advertising to one or more whole areas, rather than to specific addresses, you should find the Household Delivery Service useful. This arranges for your advertising to be delivered by the regular postmen on their rounds. The charge for this to you is based on the weight of the material: there are two weight categories, with a 60g maximum.

Six weeks' advance booking is required and depends on post-code area availability. The more you send, the lower the rates.

The Royal Mail also offers Mailsort, a range of discount services for presorted mail which apply to bulk mailings of 4,000 or more letters or 1,000 or more packets, provided these have been sorted in advance by the sender, according to postcode.

Bear in mind, however, that you will have to pay someone to do the sorting, so these services are unlikely to prove useful to you until your business has expanded greatly.

Further details of these and other services can be obtained from the customer care unit at your local district/head post office.

Mailing lists

You do not, of course, write to the population at large; you need a mailing list of people likely to be interested.

If you want to sell to an industry or trade, you can make up your own mailing list out of entries in the trade directories; this is laborious but relatively inexpensive.

It is more effective if you can find out the name of each firm's buyer – from a trade reference book, the appropriate trade association or by telephoning the firm – and address the letter individually to him or her, making it appear unique. This is easy if you can get your letters prepared on a word processor.

If your customer information is kept on computer files, then it is subject to the Data Protection Act 1984, which is concerned with regulating the use of information about living individuals that is held on computer (personal data). The Act places obligations upon those that hold and use personal data (data users). Data users must be open about that use by registering under the Act, and they are bound by the eight Data Protection Principles contained within it. Full details can be obtained from the Office of the Data Protection Registrar, Wycliffe House, Water Lane, Wilmslow, Cheshire SK9 5AF   TEL (0625) 535777.

For advertising to local firms, relevant names and addresses from *Yellow Pages* can be used in the same way.

For advertising to individual consumers, you can try to make up your own mailing list from the electoral register.

Many organisations have subscription or membership lists that they may be willing to rent out to you, for a fee. If the list is very large, they may agree to let you have part of it, or even just a very small part, so that you can test how well the list works for your purposes. Do not be too surprised, however, if the part that you are offered for the test turns out to be the best part of the list. To get a fairer idea of how useful the list is going to be to you, ask for a cross-selection – say, one out of every six names. A large percentage of any full list is likely to be postally undeliverable – 'no such address' or 'gone away'.

You may be able to buy the list, in which case you will receive the names and addresses and can use them as often as you like, for whatever purpose you like. However, very few organisations sell their lists; they rather rent them out or exchange lists. Exchanging means that two organisations use each others' lists – but you, as a beginner, will not have anything to swap.

The organisation may make it a condition to have sight of and approve the offer which is to be mailed. To prevent you from copying their lists, they may insist that the addressing and posting are done by a specialist mailing company.

You will, of course, learn the names and addresses of those who reply, and they then become part of your own list, which you later may sell, rent out or exchange. There are a number of list brokers who may be able to help you find lists, for a fee.

Counting the cost

First calculate the likely cost, and be clear how to assess the responses. 25p per name and address may not sound much, but if the response rate is one per cent, the cost becomes £25 per reply.

The response rate to direct mail advertising is variable, depending on the product, the market and the care taken in preparation: a response of between 3 and 5 per cent should be considered as extremely good. Naturally, not every enquiry results in an order; after your first mail shot you should be able to calculate whether the resulting business has earned back its promotion costs plus some profit.

Leaflet distribution is a humbler, localised version of direct mail. At its simplest, this could be a leaflet pushed through a few hundred neighbourhood doors by hired teenagers or an active retired person. You may be able to arrange for the newsagent to slip a leaflet inside every newspaper delivered, for a fee.

If you want to cover larger or more distant areas, you would have to entrust the work to a specialist firm: look in *Yellow Pages* under Addressing/Circularising Services, and Circular/Sample Distributors.

Thomson Directories publishes a series of booklets to help the advertising novice. *Small Business Guide to Advertising* gives useful advice on planning every kind of advertising campaign, and includes a summary of all the main advertising media. Others in the series are *A Guide to Better Business on the Telephone* and *Better Results from Advertising in Directories*. The booklets are free from the Customer Care Department, Thomson Directories, 296 Farnborough Road, Farnborough, Hampshire GU14 7NU TEL (0252) 516111.

Mailing Preference Service

The use of direct mail is a very effective form of advertising, but it needs to be used with particular care. Many members of the public resent receiving mail addressed to them by name from a company with whom they have had no contact and of whom they may not have heard. They are then very likely simply to throw away what they consider to be 'junk mail', without a second glance. It is therefore in the advertiser's interest to subscribe to the Mailing Preference Service, Freepost 22, London W1E 7EZ   TEL 071-738 1625. The MPS makes available to the companies which subscribe to it a quarterly listing of people who have positively requested that they should not be sent any direct mail advertising. It also makes available a list of those people who have asked to be sent more details of goods available in some particular category. If you do your mailing through a list broker or a mailing house, make sure that they use an 'MPS–cleaned' list.

Press releases

Any event of special interest in your firm, such as the opening of a new workshop or the launching of a new product, should be communicated to the local and trade press in the form of a press release. Do not be intimidated by 'press release' – all you have to do is find out who is in charge of the, say, technical page of the newspaper and then write to them with a suitable small article. Make sure that the relevant details – the name of the product, your name, your address, the prices are included. The better and more concise manner in which it is written, the more likely it is to get in. Pictures help, but they should be black and white. If what you send catches editorial attention, and secures a paragraph or two of editorial copy, this is often more effective than any advertisement. If you place an advertisement at the same time, you may get an editorial mention – but the two are not invariably linked.

To get mentioned in the national press is helpful for anyone selling by mail order. Try to think of people who would be interested in your story, such as the women's page editor.

Selling

You will need to consider the question of distribution and selling long before you can manufacture enough to satisfy widespread demand.

Selling to shops

At the most basic level, this is a question of taking round a sample of your product to appropriate shops in the district and persuading them to stock it. To go about this sensibly, you need to:

- make an appointment to see the shop's owner or manager; do not simply turn up unannounced at the busiest time
- make yourself familiar with competing products, their prices and their drawbacks, so that you can point out the advantages of yours (without obvious knocking)
- be clear about the price of your product, but be willing to allow the retailer an attractive discount. The real problem is to decide whether to sell on sale or return, or not. On the whole, it is better not to, but if you find that one particular line does not move and others do, you could offer to buy it back in order to get the shop to take more of the merchandise that does sell
- be prepared to prove that you can guarantee supplies and will stick to delivery dates
- have the product or range of your products properly packaged, as it will look when displayed in a shop window or on a shelf
- sometimes it also helps to offer a small display aid, to show your product to its best advantage. Make clear to the shop

owner that this is on loan to display your product, not a gift, nor for use to show off someone else's goods.

The technique for larger shops, or chain stores, is to start by contacting the appropriate buyer in each store. The retail directory (from a reference library) gives some names; find out others by telephoning. Make an appointment to see each buyer.

- Pay particular attention to the presentation of your product.
- Know your maximum capacity and the size of orders you can guarantee to deliver and your most dependable delivery dates.
- Be prepared to prove that you can finance your increased output.
- When you come to discuss the price, be sure to have some room for negotiating. But remember, some large shops will expect extended credit terms and will delay payment.

Most large companies pay on a 30-day account: that is, they pay invoices on their first accounting day occurring when 30 days have passed from receipt of the invoice. (That is why it is important to invoice customers promptly and correctly, offering no excuse for delaying payment.)

If you negotiate a major contract, ask for stage payments: for instance, part payment with the order and then percentage payments at various stages of production or delivery.

Pricing

The price you charge for a product or service can be arrived at in various ways. Economists have theories about price based on cost, based on competition, based on the demand, based on the going rate; in real life for a small business, these categories tend to slide into each other.

Pricing based on costs is a crude but still commonly used method. The price is made up of the cost of the product to the manufacturer (labour, materials, overheads) plus a percentage mark-up to give what you consider to be a fair profit. Your own costs will set the lower limit.

This method, however, ignores two important factors: demand and competition. Unless you are selling bread during a famine, demand will set an upper limit on what you can charge, and so will the presence in the market of competitors.

You must allow for discounts for quantity orders, or for payment in seven days and for anything else that might encourage greater purchase or quicker settlement.

If you sell to the final consumer, by retail or through mail order, there is no problem with getting payment; but if you sell to another firm, you will need to offer credit – because the competition does – and you must cost that in.

If you sell through a wholesaler your price must allow for the wholesaler's and retailer's profit as well as your own. The price to the customer will contain the three elements of the wholesaler's mark-up, the retailer's mark-up and your profit (plus VAT if applicable). You must allow for these in order not to price yourself out of the market.

Pricing based on competition
It is important to identify your competitors and to make yourself familiar with what they are offering at what prices. You can, to a large extent, be guided by what competitors are asking for a comparable product.

For most products there are several price ranges, and manufacturers deliberately tailor their goods to fit into one of these. Some manufacturers produce several product ranges, each one for a different category. Cosmetics, for instance, tend to be cheap and cheerful for the young, medium priced for the average user, and extremely expensive for the richer consumer. You should decide at an early stage into which price category your product will slot.

If you cannot fit into the lower or middle range, because your costs are high, you will have to aim at the higher category; but then you will have to make sure that the prices reflect some special and unique quality of your goods, and show the customer that this is so. There are some categories of goods – cosmetics, again, are an example – where a high price can actually be a selling point: the customer is reassured by it that she is getting a unique, luxury article, and it would be an error of psychology to charge less.

Another way of taking demand into account is this. If you produce a range of related goods, some will be more in demand than others: your pricing should therefore be based on a profit margin averaged out over the whole range.

Or you may try loss-leader pricing of one or more items, at cost, or very little above it, as a bait to capture a large share of the market quickly. But you will be the baiter bit if you sell all the low-profit items and none of the high-profit ones.

Pricing based on the going rate incorporates the elements of competition and of demand. It is the way of pricing in most service industries. Where there is no going rate, you must cost your own time very carefully when calculating your overheads. But, usually, there is a recognised going rate for the service, and in order to charge more, you would need to offer something out of the ordinary: such as being on call at all hours, or having unusually high qualifications, or offering a particularly comprehensive service.

Face-to-face selling

Many people who would find no difficulty in selling goods across a shop counter, feel deeply embarrassed when it comes to calling on firms to offer their goods or services.

Aggressive selling is, however, rarely required: one's best weapon is a detailed knowledge of one's project and a readiness to explain it fluently, even demonstrate it.

Present as good an appearance as possible: as a small entrepreneur you will inspire more confidence by a show of frugal efficiency than by lavish trimmings. (For some kinds of service only, such as consultancy perhaps, appearances are important, since you may have nothing else to show your client.)

Keep good records of your customers, how much they buy and when – a computer could prove useful there. Keep in constant touch, so that when they think of buying, you are in the forefront of their minds. Ask them if they are satisfied, and treat complaints in a friendly spirit; look into the complaint and put right anything that needs rectifying.

Genuinely listen to what the potential customer says, and show an obvious interest in what he or she wants.

In many cases you must be able to offer a service, as well as a product: installation, spare parts and servicing. Make sure that you have the facilities for this, or next time the customer may go elsewhere. If you cannot provide the service yourself, find a sub-contractor.

Know your potential customer's own products and be able to discuss them intelligently, and if you yourself happen to use his competitor's product, keep this to yourself.

Employing an agent

If you dislike or have no talent for selling, or do not have time for it, you may be better occupied concentrating on the production side, while getting someone else to sell for you. You might think of persuading a golden-tongued friend to do you the favour, if only for the initial contacting, but a proper business partner, or, best of all for this purpose, a proper agent, is preferable.

The advantages for a new business can be considerable. An agent will have the necessary contacts, and be known in the trade; he or she can also keep you informed about what your competitors are doing. Your agent will need to be primed with any necessary technical information and supplied with promotional literature, possibly backed with advertising.

The disadvantage is that the agent's commission reduces your profit margin – but perhaps you would not have had the profit at all, but for him or her.

An agent usually represents more than one firm, and you can never guarantee that the agent is trying as hard for you as for the others: he or she naturally works hardest for products offering the highest return.

To find an agent, consult one or all of these: the trade press; trade directories; *Yellow Pages* (under Manufacturers' Agents and Marketing Consultants); or advertise for one yourself. You can negotiate any agreement that seems suitable, but both the agent and you must be quite clear about the terms before starting.

Mail order selling

Direct response mail order selling is a system in which press advertisements urge customers to order goods, which are then sent to them directly.

Payment is usually by cash (cheque) with order or by credit card; it is usual to offer free approval ('money back if not delighted') which is required by most of the relevant codes of practice. Some firms offer credit terms, but these are usually catalogue mail order houses rather than firms selling their own products.

To be suitable for mail order selling, the product should fall into one or more of the following categories:

- light in weight and strong enough not to break in transit, *or* bulky but capable of being compactly and securely packed (for example, many types of garden sheds and greenhouses are sold by mail order);
- not obtainable in ordinary retail shops, that is, in some way new, unique or hard to find – for example a craft product, or something for a minority taste, *or* obtainable in shops, but at a much higher price. Make sure, however, that the customer's postage costs do not take away your price advantage. Because of postage, very low-priced articles are not worth selling by mail.

Your customers must be left in no doubt about the total cost of any goods offered. In particular, make clear whether the costs of packing and postage or delivery are included in the price, and if not, what these costs are.

Not only your production but your packing, despatch and administration must be up to scratch. Before starting the operation be sure that you have the stocks and the extra capacity to meet a sudden increase in demand, and are able to deliver goods within the promised period. This should be within 28 days. If you suddenly find that an order cannot be sent off within the period you promised, you should immediately contact the buyer and offer a refund; or if the customer chooses to wait, he or she should be given a firm date for the despatch of the order.

These points, and very many others with which you must comply in this form of selling, are contained in the code of practice of the Direct Marketing Association Ltd., Haymarket House, 1 Oxendon Street, London SW1Y 4EE   TEL 071-321 2525. The DMA code is binding only on members of the Association.

It follows, and reproduces much of, the British Code of Advertising Practice which is administered by the Advertising Standards Authority alongside the British Code of Sales Promotion Practice and which can be obtained free of charge from the ASA.

You must conform to both the legal requirements and the voluntary codes of practice governing mail order selling. And to advertise in the national press you must get clearance from the National Newspapers' Mail Order Protection Scheme Ltd. TEL 071-405 6806, which runs a Mail Order Protection Scheme (MOPS) jointly with the Incorporated Society of British Advertisers and the Institute of Practitioners in Advertising. You must pay an annual fee to a central fund which indemnifies readers against loss due to a firm's failure to supply goods ordered if they are liquidated or cease to trade. If you are approved to join, you must display the MOPS logo in your advertisement.

Similar schemes are operated by many local papers. To advertise in magazines you will need to comply with the conditions of the Mail Order Protection Scheme as operated by members of the Periodical Publishers Association. Unlike the NPA MOPS, the PPA scheme is not centrally run, nor funded by contributions from advertisers. Instead, each individual publisher requires would-be advertisers to complete application forms asking for details of their business. On the basis of this information, a judgement is made as to whether the applicants should be allowed to solicit money off the page in the publications. Further details of the PPA scheme can be obtained from the Periodical Publishers Association, Imperial House, 15-19 Kingsway, London WC2B 6UN TEL 071-379 6268.

Linage advertising in the classified columns is exempt from the MOPS stipulations, but you still have to get your advertising copy cleared. It must, in any event, conform to the British Code of Advertising Practice. To ensure that your advertisement will be acceptable, contact the Advertising Standards Authority: its Code of Advertising Practice secretariat will give you (confidential) advice and discuss your proposals with you.

The ASA's address is Brook House, 2–16 Torrington Place, London WC1E 7HN TEL 071-580 5555 and that of the National Newspaper Mail Order Protection Scheme is 16 Tooks Court, London EC4A 1LB TEL 071-405 6806.

Make sure that you have an efficient system (perhaps on computer) for recording the product sold, the dates of purchase and despatch, and the name and address of each customer (which is then added to your own mailing list). Note, however, that if you process personal data of this type you must register the uses, classes, sources and disclosures of this data with the Data Protection Registrar and comply with the eight Data Protection Principles. It is a criminal offence to collect or use personal data without having registered. In addition, industry guidelines on direct marketing, including list and database practice, are contained within the British Code of Advertising Practice, available from the Advertising Standards Authority, Brook House, 2–16 Torrington Place, London WC1E 7HN   TEL 071-580 5555.

As with direct mail advertising, ask the postal services representative about reduced terms for bulk parcel despatch.

If you advertise in several newspapers and magazines, it is worth using a simple code to distinguish replies from each source, so that you can tell which one brings in the most business.

The price you charge for your product must take into account the advertising costs – often as much as one third of the selling price – as well as the cost of replacing damaged articles, and, if you offer credit, of bad debts. If you sell on credit, or free approval, allow for this in your cash flow forecasting.

Providing credit card facilities may be worthwhile, since it allows the customer to obtain credit without risk to yourself – your money is guaranteed, provided you adhere to the conditions.

If you are interested in accepting cards, telephone the local card area sales office (address from the head office, or your local telephone directory) to obtain details. If necessary, they will arrange for a representative to call to discuss the arrangements. There is a service charge or commission of up to 5 per cent, plus, in most cases, an initial fee of £50 to £60.

Because in mail order selling there is no customer's signature on the credit card slip, you have to enter the details (customer's card number and its expiry date, the name and address, the address for delivery, amount charged) and send this schedule to the headquarters of the card company, or else take it to your bank. Your account will be credited with the full amount; you

will receive a monthly statement from the card company, showing the service charge due, and you will pay this by direct debit.

Selling in a very small way

Market stalls and country fairs provide an outlet for a small
business making a slow, cautious start at selling, and are particularly suited to craft goods. The local authority who do the
licensing of stalls will be able to tell you where and when fairs are
held in the district, and how to rent a stall, either permanently or
by the day.

Exhibiting at a local craft fair could be a good way of launching
a product. Some craft associations will arrange to exhibit members' work. The *Showman's Directory* (TEL (0483) 422184) will
give you a list of non-craft events throughout the country, which
might be of use in finding appropriate locations for selling or
publicity; it will also tell you where to hire marquees and other
equipment.

CHAPTER 5

PREMISES

THE question of premises obviously varies according to the type of business. The kind of space you need to work in will depend largely on whether you manufacture goods, or sell them, or offer a service.

Advice about the regulations

Offices, shops, factories and many other types of commercial accommodation have to comply with regulations about the safety of staff and facilities for them; so it is as well to be sure that one's prospective premises either accord with the regulations, or are capable of being converted so as to comply with them. Information about this can be obtained from the Health and Safety Executive's enquiry point at Broad Lane, Sheffield S3 7HQ TEL (0742) 768141. There is also a free leaflet line: TEL (0742) 892346.

When you contact the HSE you should ask for the Library and Information Services. You can also get this information from the planning department of your local authority.

Premises for a service industry

If you provide a service, for example as a builder, decorator or plumber, probably all of your work will be carried on in your customers' premises. To begin with you will only need some space at home in which to do the paperwork, and perhaps a shed or garage for storing tools. However, if your business thrives and grows, and you come to employ workers, you will eventually need an office to deal with enquiries, estimates and paperwork, and also larger storage space, and parking for your vans – proper business premises, in fact.

If your business is a consultancy or agency needing little or no equipment, you may require only a room or two and find it convenient to make over some part of your house to business use, or you may choose to rent a small office somewhere else. The physical location of your office may not be crucial to your success.

Obviously, for a very small and new business there is a tremendous advantage in working from home: you save on rent, rates, cost of the public utilities, cleaning – and even staff, if a member of your family answers the door and the telephone and perhaps does the typing.

However, some house deeds prohibit use for business purposes, and many restrictive covenants of this type would be enforceable. Even where there are no such restrictions, if you carry on a business from residential premises, you may need planning permission from the local authority and may have to pay higher charges for commercial occupation. You should, in any event, inform the company that is insuring your house. Using it for business, particularly if you are storing any combustible goods, may invalidate the buildings and contents insurance – even against totally unrelated disasters, such as a burst water pipe.

There are plenty of small businesses run inconspicuously from home without permission because there is nothing in the work to inconvenience the neighbours or to alert snoopers. But if you want to be above-board in carrying on your business, or if your house needs to be altered in any way for the purpose, as in adding a room or shed, you may need planning permission. There is a fee payable when an application for planning permission is submitted to the local authority.

If you claim a proportion of the expenses of running your home as a business expense, there is a risk of your having to pay capital gains tax on the same proportion of the gains realised when you eventually sell the house. A small gain may well fall within your exempt allowance for the year in which you sell, but be sure to check the position with your accountant.

The permission may be qualified by some conditions relating to hours of work, or callers at the house. If your application is refused, you have the right to appeal, but if this fails, you may have no choice but to look elsewhere for accommodation.

Premises for a manufacturing business

Unless you are a craftsman working single-handed and in a very small business, it is unlikely that you will be able to work from home: apart from probable lack of workshop space, you may well run into opposition from the local authority or neighbours.

A manufacturing firm has to satisfy zoning regulations for light and heavy industry, because it may create noise, smoke, fumes, industrial waste that must be disposed of, other sorts of environmental pollution; or it may increase the risk of fire. It is extremely unlikely that you could carry on a manufacturing business clandestinely, or that you would get permission to do so in residential premises.

As for renting workshop space, at the present time there are many millions of square feet of factory premises vacant in Britain, but only a small percentage of this is suitable for a business which is just starting up. Just the same, there is no reason why you should not get hold of some of this percentage if you go about it the right way.

Hunting for workshop space

Define your exact requirements. You will need a site big enough to allow your firm to settle down and expand, because you may not want to have to move in a year or two. There must be access to all the mains services; warehousing space; room and amenities for the workers; parking space; room for lorries to load and unload. You probably do not need a central situation or a street frontage, but you must ensure that any noise, fumes, smoke, do not annoy people living nearby, especially during overtime working.

You may need an office if you expect customers to be calling on you. There may be a number of other requirements: it is unlikely that any one site will satisfy all of them.

Begin by applying to the local authority. Some authorities try to cater for the very small business by building 'nursery' units, which are simply shells, sometimes only 500 square feet (about the size of a double garage). The cost of building these is high, and so, consequently, are the rents. But, if the authority is anxious to promote employment, it may offer you a short period rent-free.

The local authority may also give you favourable rental terms, or even a rent-free period, if it wants you out of a mainly residential area where your activities are unwelcome and you are what is called a 'non-conformer user', and the neighbours (can be persuaded to) campaign for your removal or closure.

Some councils keep a register of vacant industrial property, and may be able to help you by extracting from this a list of suitable properties. Most local authorities recognise that their attitude to small business can affect unemployment levels, and are as helpful as they can be. You may also be able to get information and advice from your local enterprise agency.

But if official bodies cannot help, you must make the rounds of the estate agents. If you do resort to these, remember that they may need telephoning at intervals to remind them of your existence. Low-cost, low-rental premises have little value to an agent because they bring in a low fee. Very small and cheap premises in the centre of town do not always reach the estate agents' lists, so keep your own eyes open, and also study the classified advertisements in the local press.

When you find a place that seems suitable, there are still a number of factors to be considered, for instance, whether to buy or to lease.

While some business premises are sold freehold, the majority of them are only available on lease. For someone starting in business, a lease has the considerable advantage of being relatively inexpensive to acquire and of not necessarily calling for a long-term commitment. Most leasehold premises that are available for sale comprise existing leases. Here the terms are not negotiable (they are already set out in the lease) and you must either accept the whole 'package' or hunt for other premises. Sometimes premises may be available on a new lease; the terms may be negotiable to some extent, although this will not be the case if, for example, you are taking a lease of a new industrial unit where the landlord is insisting on uniform terms applying to each tenant.

There can be a substantial difference between a new and an existing lease in terms of cost of purchase. A tenant selling a lease will usually ask for a 'premium' (a capital sum) to be paid by the incoming tenant, and this will be determined by market forces. A lease at a low rent can attract a considerable premium, whereas one with very little time to run may be difficult to sell and thus warrant little or no premium. A tenant anxious to sell may even pay his or her buyer a 'reverse premium' to take over the lease. By contrast, it is unusual for a premium to be called for by a landlord on the grant of a new lease; a tenant may expect instead to have to bear his or her legal costs for granting it. Where a tenant is required by a new lease to spend money on fitting out the premises, it may be appropriate for him or her to ask for a rent-free period as recompense.

You will minimise your responsibilities by acquiring premises on as short a lease as possible. This is not difficult in the case of buying a suitable existing lease. But what are your rights if you want to stay on at the premises once the lease has come to an end?

Ideally your lease would give you a right to a new lease if you so wish. However, few landlords are prepared to tie their hands in this way. A tenant of business premises does have a right to apply to the court for the grant of a new lease (with some minor exceptions) but the landlord may object on certain grounds. It will thus never be certain that a tenant will succeed in obtaining a new lease against his landlord's opposition. In practice, however, the vast majority of such cases are settled by negotiation.

Business leases are highly technical documents: do not try to do your own conveyancing, it could cost you dear. Employ a solicitor experienced in this field.

It is unwise to rent or buy a building without first having a survey done; you might have unpleasant surprises later, when structural or other faults may come to light. If the survey sounds expensive, talk to the surveyor about a negotiated fee. You do not want a lengthy catalogue listing features that you can see for yourself, nor a full unlimited guarantee on which you could sue if the surveyor missed anything. What you want is a realistic guide to the value of the property and what you must do to it soon, what you can risk leaving for a while, and what is unimportant structurally. Such information is as useful given orally as it would be in a typed document, and is far cheaper, especially if it is without the insurance-underwritten indemnity.

If the property is an older one which you will have to refurbish at your own expense, you will be increasing its value to the owner, so you may be able to negotiate a cheaper rent.

Check that there will be no difficulties with the mains services, that there will be enough electric power, water, gas, and also adequate drainage, and no difficulties about the telephone.

Somebody who is a low user of water should ask the water undertaking or water authority to be allowed to be metered instead of being charged a fixed rate.

Fire prevention

Premises require a fire certificate if they are used as a place of work, a shop, factory or office where more than 20 people are employed, or more than 10 people elsewhere than on the ground floor; or if explosives or highly inflammable substances are stored there.

If you are moving into previously occupied premises, find out whether there is a current fire certificate, and if so, whether it covers your operations. If your occupancy constitutes a change of conditions because of structural alterations, a change of use, or change in the number of persons working, you will need a new certificate.

Your local fire prevention officer grants the certificate if he or she is satisfied, after inspecting the premises, that all necessary precautions have been taken.

Consult your fire prevention officer before you clinch the deal for any premises: if your work means installing a number of fire escapes, fire doors, new flooring, this may prove to be too expensive to be worthwhile. You cannot argue with fire prevention officers: their word is law with no appeal, and you can be closed down without notice. You may find that until you have satisfied the demands of fire prevention, you will be refused any other kind of permission that may also be required.

Even if you do not need a fire certificate, your premises must have adequate means of escape, and fire-fighting equipment.

Planning permission

Make sure that the premises you choose already have the planning permission that you will need. Otherwise you will have to apply to the local authority's planning department for permission to make alterations or to change the use of the premises. Obtaining this can take months (and there are fees to be paid). If you take the local authority's planners into your confidence from the start, they may prove remarkably helpful, and eager not to thwart a new business, unless there are overwhelming objections to the plans you put forward.

If you intend to start from a green-field site and build on it, planning permission will take much longer, and is only one of the obstacles to be overcome.

A free booklet, *A Step-by-Step Guide to Planning Permission for Small Businesses*, is available from the Department of the Environment, 2 Marsham Street, London SW1P 3EB   TEL 071-276 3000 or from Welsh Office Planning Division, New Crown Building, Cathays Park, Cardiff CF1 3NQ   TEL (0222) 825111.

Rates and concessions

If you are not tied to any one area and can set up anywhere, you may be better off in an assisted area, where you may sometimes get rent-free accommodation for up to two years, perhaps in a purpose-built factory.

English Estates provides a wide range of ready-made industrial and commercial premises with a wide range of helpful tenancy terms throughout the assisted areas of England. It operates from 15 offices around the country; full details are available from the head office, St George's House, Kingsway, Team Valley, Gateshead, Tyne & Wear NE11 0NA   TEL 091-487 8941.

Many local authorities are prepared to give initial rate relief to new businesses and those relocating themselves into the area. Get in touch with the planning department or the economic unit of your local authority about these or other concessions.

If you intend to set up a business in a rural area, consult the local Rural Development Commission Business Service (see page 27) which may know of small properties, converted barns, or other accommodation available for rent.

Sublet premises

If you need only a modest amount of space, you may be able to find an existing business which has spare capacity, and is glad to reduce its overheads by subletting to you. The kind of business to look for is one in a similar but not competing line of business: the association could even result in a partnership.

CHAPTER 6

SQUARING UP TO ACCOUNTS

THE FIGURES that your business generates are an index of its health and growth. Many people in a small business seem to be positively scared of them and keep no continuous control.

It is not good enough to monitor the state of health of the business by the annual accounts, which are not available until the following year is well advanced. If anything is then found to be amiss, it may well be too late to put it right.

You may feel that if you employ an accountant, it is his or her job to keep an eye on the figures, on the why-keep-a-dog-and-bark-yourself? principle. But an accountant should rather be thought of as a doctor who cannot compel you to look after your business health properly, but can only diagnose the sickness resulting from your imprudence. He or she certainly cannot cure it once it has become terminal.

So, do not be scared of your accounts and take an informed interest in what the figures show you.

You should know at the end of each month, if not every week, whether it has been a profitable one, and whether you have enough money, in hand or on tap, to cover your expenses for the coming month. Your calculations need not be very elaborate: quite rough monthly accounts, backed up by an accountant's quarterly report, will enable you to stay in control.

For advice on how to find an accountant, see page 44.

What you can do for yourself

Your accountant could, of course, carry out your monthly monitoring for you; but it is most unlikely that your new, small business could afford the expense. If you do this work for yourself, you will be in a position to know, at all times, what is happening to your business, and to forecast what is going to happen next.

What is more, you will then have no trouble in understanding the accountant's quarterly reports, and relating them to your own day-to-day experience. Even if you prefer to have your accountant do all the figure work, you must be able to make sense of the reports that are prepared for you.

Keeping business records

There are excellent reasons why you should keep good business records: because the Inland Revenue and Customs and Excise (for VAT) require it, because your bank manager may require regular information, and because you will save your accountant's time (charged for by the hour). But the most important reason is that properly kept accounts, summarised at the end of each month and coupled with a stocktake or an estimate of the value of your stock, will give you the up-to-date knowledge of your affairs which you need to spot danger signs while there is still time to put things right, and to plan ahead for further improvements or expansion, if things go well.

Who keeps the books?

Although all modern double-entry bookkeeping follows the same general pattern, no two firms' sets of books are identical: every business has some individual aspects which must be recorded, and every businessman or businesswoman has his or her own notions of which of these records should be monitored.

So get your accountant, who understands your particular requirements, to set up your books for you, and to teach you how to keep them. He or she will probably do so willingly, for it is to his or her advantage, as well as yours, to be presented with clear, well-kept books to deal with. Or, better still, ask your book-keeper to teach some member of your family whom you can conscript to relieve you of the task. It is not difficult, and it will probably be some time before your business demands the services of a full-time trained bookkeeper.

You can also teach yourself the elements of bookkeeping from one of a variety of books on the subject, but be sure to acquire this skill before you start up, because you will not have time afterwards.

The records you must keep

Business records may be kept and presented in a variety of ways, and depend very much on the type of business for their format.

However, one feature is common to all systems: they must be backed by evidence that the receipts and payments recorded have actually been made. So be sure to keep safely all of the following:

- cheque-book stubs
- cancelled cheques (tell the bank to return them to you)
- bank paying-in books (use them, not paying-in slips)
- bank statements (make sure that you have separate accounts – even if they are at the same bank – for business and private life, whether you are sole trader or partnership or company)
- copies of your own invoices, receipts and delivery notes
- your suppliers' invoices, receipts and delivery notes
- receipts, wherever possible, for minor purchases made in cash
- copies of VAT returns.

The books

For keeping accounts, even at their simplest, you must keep several books.

The cash book is the most basic account book. It records all your payments and receipts made by cheque (for this purpose cheques are regarded as cash) or in ready money.

Some businesses are purely cash ones – this means that, whether you are buying or selling, payment is made immediately. If yours is not one of these, and you buy and sell with payment at a later date, you will need two further books, a sales day book for recording your sales invoices as they are sent out, and a purchases day book in which are recorded your purchases of goods and services.

This last book, which is all-important, will be of the kind called an analysis book, ruled with a number of vertical columns, in which you classify your different kinds of expenditure: materials, direct labour and the various sorts of overheads. Be sure to get a book with enough columns; how many you will need depends on your particular expenses, and on how minutely you want to break the figures down.

By adding up each column every month, you will see exactly how much each of your business expenses came to. The total of these totals will give you your whole month's costs. If you are registered for VAT, you will have a VAT column in both your sales and your purchases books, to record the amount of VAT that other people pay you, and that which you pay; this information you will need for your quarterly VAT return.

If you employ anyone you must keep a record of wages paid, showing gross earnings, deductions for income tax, National Insurance, any pension scheme, any other deductions, net pay and the employer's National Insurance contributions. You can obtain a proprietary wages book system from a business stationer. If you decide to use a computer in your business, you can buy a program that will attend to the wages records for you.

The petty cash book is a record of small out-of-pocket expenses paid by you or your staff in the course of work. It may include any number of different things, such as fares, taxis, the window cleaner and the tea bought for tea-breaks. The money is paid out of a float drawn at intervals from the bank (and duly recorded in the cash and purchase books). The petty cash book is on the same lines as the purchases book, with columns for different sorts of expenditure.

Slightly more advanced bookkeeping

As your business expands and becomes more complex, you will need to start keeping ledgers.

The sales ledger is based on the sales day book, and records the individual accounts of each of your customers, showing how much he or she has bought in any given period and the date of payments. This enables you to keep an eye on slow payers. (It is also invaluable in planning future marketing strategy. It may show, for instance, that 80 per cent of your trade is with a few customers placing substantial orders, and 20 per cent is with a large number of small customers. You will then have to decide whether to go on accepting small orders whose costs are high in relation to the profits, in the hope that the small customers may be encouraged to grow into bigger ones.)

The purchases ledger is based on the purchases day book, and records your transactions with each of your suppliers. It shows which of them are getting the largest share of your custom; these will be the ones most likely to give credit or offer generous cash discounts.

The general ledger records impersonal payments, that is, the sale and purchase of equipment, rent and rates, services, etc, and the totals of income and expenditure.

These ledgers are the foundation for a double-entry bookkeeping system. A full explanation of this would require a book to itself, but the principle on which it is based is a simple one: it is that every transaction must be recorded twice, once as a debit and once as a credit, according to whether it is regarded from a buyer's or a seller's point of view.

Every sale you make represents a debit entry to your customer in the sales ledger and a credit to you in the sales account in the general ledger: when the customer pays, this appears as a debit entry in the cash book and a credit entry in the sales ledger.

Every purchase you make from your supplier is a credit entry for him or her in your purchases ledger and a debit for you in the general ledger. When you pay up, this is recorded as a credit in your cash book and a debit for the supplier in the purchases ledger.

Using what your figures tell you

With all these records, you are in a position to make calculations showing how your business is progressing. The all-important one is your monthly net profit. To arrive at this you need to draw up a monthly trading account and a profit and loss account. The monthly trading account shows the gross profits of your business. You calculate it by adding together your month's labour and materials costs, and the difference between the value of your opening and closing stocks, and subtracting this from the total monthly sales figure.

Jane's product sells at £20 per unit; of this, her materials cost £10 and labour costs £2. Her overheads are £800 a month. Using the sales, purchase and labour totals shown by her books, Jane draws up a trading account, thus:

JANE'S TRADING ACCOUNT FOR ONE MONTH

	£		£
Opening stock		Sales	4,000
(100 units @ £12)	1,200		
Purchases of materials			
(200 @ £10)	2,000		
Labour (200 @ £2)	400		
	3,600		
Less closing stock			
(80 @ £12)	960		
	2,640		
Balance, i.e. gross			
profit	1,360		
	4,000		4,000

Jane has valued her stock at materials and labour costs only: overheads do not enter the calculation until the next step, the monthly estimated net profit. This is how it looks in Jane's case:

JANE'S PROFIT AND LOSS ACCOUNT

	£		£
Overheads	800	Gross	
		profit	1,360
Balance, i.e.			
net profit	560		
	1,360		1,360

This is the most basic way of drawing up a profit and loss account. It can, in fact, be combined with the trading account in a single calculation. There is no special presentation that must be followed.

You can make it more informative by making it more complex: you can isolate and thus spotlight items of overheads or other factors that you particularly want to keep an eye on, for instance, the cost of power consumption. Or, because power is a cost that varies with the volume of production, you could choose to treat it as a materials purchase, rather than an overhead.

Here we have assumed that Jane's enterprise is a limited company and her salary is therefore one of the overheads. If she were a sole trader, her remuneration (say, £350 a month) would not be included in the overheads, which would then be £450 a month, and the month's net profit before tax would be £910, and would constitute Jane's taxable income.

However, you may have a profit and loss account that looks as healthy as this one, and still run out of funds, because it does not show that at any one time you may not actually have in hand all the money due to you. If your suppliers demand cash on delivery while your customers will only place orders on 30- or 60-day credit terms, and your expanding business is demanding additional unforeseen expenditure, you have got a cash flow problem.

Cash flow forecasting

The drawing up of a cash flow forecast has already been explained. In the examples that follow, the tables are considerably simplified; in particular, they ignore VAT and assume equal monthly overheads.

Jane's latest cash flow forecast looks like this (figures in brackets denote a deficit):

Month	Jan	Feb	Mar	Apr	May
	£	£	£	£	£
Opening bank balance/[overdraft] . . .	[3,000]	[2,200]	[1,400]	[600]	200
Payments:					
purchases	2,000	2,000	2,000	2,000	2,000
labour	400	400	400	400	400
overheads	800	800	800	800	800
Maximum borrowing requirement . .	6,200	5,400	4,600	3,800	3,000
Receipts from sales	4,000	4,000	4,000	4,000	4,000
Closing balance/[overdraft]	[2,200]	[1,400]	[600]	200	1,000

Jane has now been asked to take on a regular order for another 200 units a month, but with payment only after 90 days. This means another machine at £500, plus additional part-time labour costs, and it will take two months to build up the manufacturing capacity. In order to be in a position to decide whether to accept the order, Jane prepares another forecast, which looks like this:

CASH FLOW FORECAST II
[figures in brackets denote a deficit]

Month	Jun	July	Aug	Sept	Oct	Nov	Dec
Products made	200	300	400	400	400	400	400
	£	£	£	£	£	£	£
Opening balance/ [overdraft]	1,000	300	[1,300]	[2,900]	[4,500]	[4,100]	[1,700]
Payment:							
purchases	3,000	4,000	4,000	4,000	4,000	4,000	4,000
labour	400	800	800	800	800	800	800
overheads	800	800	800	800	800	800	800
Capital expenditure . .	500						
Maximum borrowing requirement	3,700	5,300	6,900	8,500	10,100	9,700	7,300
Receipts from sales . .	4,000	4,000	4,000	4,000	6,000	8,000	8,000
Closing balance/ [overdraft]	300	[1,300]	[2,900]	[4,500]	[4,100]	[1,700]	700

It shows her that if she accepts the order under these conditions, she will be overdrawn for five months, and will need a further investment of around £4,500 for three months, to pay for the additional costs. The bank might well be willing, on the basis of this profitable order, to lend the money to a customer who had already succeeded in repaying an overdraft of £3,000. To minimise her borrowing requirement, Jane might be able to persuade her suppliers to agree to a delayed payment, and might also be able to dovetail this payment into those months when no major overheads were due.

In order to keep the example simple, two other factors have been excluded: the cost of additional power consumption resulting from increased production, and the interest payable on bank loans or overdrafts; but a rough calculation is all that is wanted at this stage.

108

Jane's experience shows that for a small, newly established firm, a large order, unaccompanied by prompt payment, can be a disaster if there is no means of stretching resources to cover the expenditure demanded by the additional output. By making a forecast on similar lines, you will be able to see how your money supply will relate to your expenditure.

Having discovered what your volume of production is to be in the next six months or so, your next task is to discover at which point you will begin to make a profit.

Break-even point

Every business has a break-even point, at which it is producing just enough for the receipts to balance the costs. Before this point is reached, the business is working at a loss; when it is passed, the business is showing a profit.

In a manufacturing business the break-even point is measured in units of production; in a service one, in the number of paid hours worked.

Fixed and variable costs

The costs of manufacturing anything can be divided into two categories: fixed and variable.

Fixed costs are the ones which remain the same whatever the amount you manufacture: the overheads and, in the short term, labour.

Variable costs are those which vary with the amount you manufacture, such as materials and power.

Some costs are partly fixed and partly variable, for example, power, which you are bound to use to some extent even without manufacturing anything: they should be split, in calculations, into their fixed and variable elements. However, in the example that follows, power has, for the sake of simplicity, been treated as an overhead.

In the case of George, another manufacturer, the relationship between his volume of production (number of units made and sold in a month) and his profitability is as follows:

Units made	Variable cost	Fixed cost	Total cost	Receipts from sales	Profit/ [loss]
20	200	1,200	1,400	400	[1,000]
60	600	1,200	1,800	1,200	[600]
100	1,000	1,200	2,200	2,000	[200]
140	1,400	1,200	2,600	2,800	200

These figures can be expressed in a graph. The horizontal axis represents the number of units produced, the vertical axis represents money. On this are plotted George's selling price and total cost at each volume of production. The two lines intersect at the point at which production is 120 units: this is where he is just covering his costs, and beyond this, he will begin to make a profit.

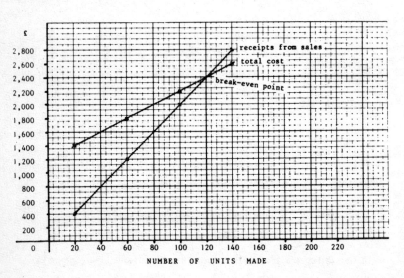

A calculation and simple graph like this will enable you to plan your volume of production intelligently in relation to your financial resources. You can use it to explore the way in which fixed costs, variable costs, sales prices and profits affect each other. For instance, you may wish to expand manufacture to an extent which will increase your fixed costs: can you maintain profits, bearing in mind your probable increase in variable costs?

Never forget to revise your cash flow forecast when you expect a change in circumstances, particularly if you are thinking of expanding production in search of higher sales.

Balance sheet

At any time after starting up, you may want to analyse your deployment of your resources: the balance sheet constitutes such an analysis. You will need – and any substantial lender will require – not just a year-end balance sheet, but also intermediate ones, or the details for them at regular intervals. You can then observe what the trend is in any particular matter that you want to analyse.

A balance sheet shows the financial state of the business at a given date and is based on the account balances in the ledgers at that date.

It takes account of what the business owns (its assets), and of what it owes (its liabilities). Both of these may be subdivided into fixed and current ones.

- Fixed liabilities are debts which are repayable over a long period of time.
- Current liabilities are those which must be repaid in the short term, such as debts to suppliers, overdrafts, and interest on loans.
- Fixed assets are property such as land, buildings, plant, machinery and vehicles. (These need to be revalued period-ically, and their book value adjusted; land and buildings tend to increase in value with inflation, while plant, machinery and vehicles depreciate and have to be replaced. It is useful to set up a sinking fund or reserve for an eventual replacement cost.)
- Current assets include customers' book debts, the value of any stock held, and money in hand or in the bank.

- Quick assets are the narrow type of current assets represented by money; by assets which can be quickly converted to money, such as Stock Exchange securities; and by some short-term book debts, where these are by customers in good standing. Raw materials are not included nor, generally, are finished goods.

From the figures for assets and liabilities you can make several kinds of analysis. For example, you can look at the ability of your business to meet its commitments. Is it solvent? That is, would it be able to pay its outside creditors in full (if necessary by selling all its assets)?

It is easier to compare balance sheet positions if you convert the actual figures into a ratio or percentage of solvency.

Another test of solvency is to see whether the business, as a going concern, can meet its current liabilities out of its current assets; again, it is usual to express this in the form of a ratio. This 'current ratio' should usually be rather better than 1:1, because not all current assets may be easily saleable, so a margin of safety is prudent.

A further test – the acid test – is to see how far current liabilities can be paid out of quick assets; expressed as the 'quick ratio', this will be less than the current ratio, and often less than 1:1. In all these tests you need to be sure that you are using up-to-date realistic sale values for the assets.

Your accountant will be able to advise you about choosing the ratios that are appropriate for your own particular business, and can also tell you about some other useful analyses that you can make.

In George's case, his resources have been as follows: £3,000 capital; an overdraft facility of £2,000, of which he is at present using only £1,200; a medium-term bank loan of £2,500 to buy plant and machinery. His profit has not been taken out, but kept in reserve to be used to buy additional plant and to provide additional working capital. The astute businessman would invest his reserves, if these were not needed immediately, which would then be entered as 'investments' on the asset side of the balance.

George's balance sheet at 1 January 1993

	£	£	£
ASSETS:			
Fixed assets:			
plant and machinery .	6,500		
motor vehicles	4,000		
	10,500		
Less hire-purchase debt .	2,000	8,500	
Current assets			
stock	1,000		
debtors	2,500	3,500	12,000
LIABILITIES:			
Medium-term bank loan 2,500			
Current liabilities:			
creditors	2,800		
overdraft	1,200	4,000	6,500
TOTAL NET ASSETS			5,500

Resources to generate these net assets are:	
George's capital introduced into business	3,000
George's undrawn profits left in business	2,500
	£5,500

Assuming that George has used realistic values for the assets, then, even in a forced sale, the business is solvent. But it cannot meet current liabilities out of current assets: there is a £500 shortfall (£4,000 as against £3,500). Even less can it meet current liabilities out of 'quick' assets: there is a £1,500 shortfall, so this balance sheet is weak. We know, however, that George has £800 unused overdraft facility, and he may possibly have extra personal funds, which he could introduce. But, on the face of it, the business depends on the continued renewal of overdraft arrangements, which makes it vulnerable.

This is only one balance sheet: a whole series of them might show that this single one gives an unusually poor impression of the business. One balance sheet a year cannot ever be informative enough.

There are many ways of presenting a balance sheet, and individual items can be more closely analysed; for instance, stock can be divided into finished stock and raw materials. If you are making your balance sheet, keep it simple to begin with; if an accountant does it for you, be sure that it is done in a form that you can understand.

The very basic balance sheet (shown on page 113) does not take account of the difference between a sole trader (or partnership) and a limited company. In actual practice, the balance sheet of a company would have to be drawn up rather differently. Its capital would have to be shown among the liabilities, because it belongs, not to the company, but to its shareholders. The same is true of the net profit on the trading account: it must ultimately be distributed among the shareholders. In a sole-trader firm or partnership, the capital investment and the profits are owned by the firm and are, therefore, assets.

Factoring

If you are in real cash flow trouble, perhaps because you have reached your bank borrowing limit and have a lot of customers owing you money, you could think about factoring. The factoring company advances you the money owing on your customers' invoices, and retains a percentage as commission when they are paid.

Consult your bank manager for the name of a suitable company. Most factoring companies are backed by clearing banks or other major financial organisations. One disadvantage is that they often take only those firms which have a turnover in excess of a set (very high) amount.

Factoring traditionally used to be a last desperate try to raise money, but is now becoming a much more acceptable and commercially viable way of raising finance.

It is still an expensive way of buying money and only to be resorted to if things are – temporarily – difficult, not as a standard way of bridging the gap between outgoings and receipts, or to ensure that slow-paying customers do not lock up your working capital.

As a rule of trading, you should do all you can to induce those who owe you money to pay as quickly as possible, while paying your own bills with as much delay as possible. In both cases, the discount for quick payment is at stake; you must either give it to your customers or forfeit it from your suppliers. But in any event, a cash discount given or forfeited is likely to cost considerably less than the factoring commission.

CHAPTER 7

TAXATION AND THE SMALL BUSINESS

WHEN YOU set up in business for yourself, you come up against taxation in several different ways. You may pay:

- income tax on your business profits, or on your share of them, if you are a sole trader or partnership
- corporation tax on your profits if yours is a limited company, and if you are in the happy situation of making some profits in excess of the directors' salaries or remuneration
- value added tax (VAT)
- National Insurance contributions.

All taxes are liable to change at any time, not only with each year's Budget. Major changes are usually publicised in the national press, and you can ask your accountant to keep you up to date. The monthly updating service of *Croner's Reference Book for the Self-employed and Smaller Business*, Croner House, London Road, Kingston upon Thames, Surrey KT2 6SR TEL 081-547 3333, can be consulted at any time for the latest figures.

The first thing to do

As soon as you are ready to start trading, you should inform:

- the inspector of taxes for your trading district
- your local Customs and Excise department (the VAT office), if there is any chance that you may want or need to be registered
- your local Department of Social Security, about National Insurance.

Look up the local offices in your telephone directory; among the useful explanatory publications which they will send you, on request, are: *Starting in Business* issued by the Board of Inland Revenue (IR28) which includes a list of relevant leaflets; *The Value Added Tax Guide* (notice 700) and leaflets entitled *Should I be Registered for VAT?*; *The Ins and Outs of VAT*; *Filling in Your VAT Return*, and leaflets dealing specifically with individual types of business are all issued by HM Customs and Excise.

Income tax

Directors of companies

If yours is a limited company, you, as one of its full-time directors, are an employee: you therefore pay income tax on your salary and on any bonus under the PAYE system, like any other employee. At the start of each trading year, you determine what your annual salary is to be, and you pay it to yourself monthly or weekly. Each time, you deduct income tax according to instructions provided by Inland Revenue, to whom you send the deducted amounts, together with National Insurance contributions from you and your employees. These payroll deductions are usually sent in every month. Sometimes they may be paid in on a quarterly basis.

Salaries need not necessarily be fixed at the start of the trading year; a review may take place part way through the year. If, at the end of the trading year, the company accounts show a profit in excess of your salary or remuneration, you have the option of taking some or all of this profit as additional salary or bonus, and deducting tax from it. If there is another director (or directors), then it will be necessary to decide how to apportion such a bonus between the directors.

You also have the opportunity of paying, out of the profits, a dividend – either instead of, or as well as a bonus. Dividends are payable to the company's shareholders (who are often also the directors), in proportion to the shares held. Where shareholders are few, payment by dividends can be attractive because, unlike salary, there is no National Insurance to pay on them. There may be an advantage in paying a dividend to the shareholders before the end of the trading year: your accountant should be able to advise you on this.

Whatever part of the profits is not taken in salary, is liable for (or, in Inland Revenue jargon, 'charged to') corporation tax. It is for you, in consultation with your accountant, to decide whether it is to your advantage to pay more income tax or more corporation tax; no general ruling is possible.

Sole traders and partnerships

If you are a sole trader, or a partnership, there is no decision to be made: the whole of your business profits are treated as sole trader's or partners' income and taxed accordingly (under Schedule D); corporation tax does not apply.

Choosing your accounting year

A firm's accounts are made up annually. This does not apply to the first trading period, which may be shorter than a year, or longer. But it is usual to call the day of the year on which you first close your books, your annual accounting date, and to go on using this day as the end of the trading year for as long as the firm continues in business. It is for you to decide which day is to be your year's end. You may make it coincide with the end of the tax (fiscal) year, i.e., 5 April; or with the end of the calendar year: or you may choose any other date at all. The Board of Inland Revenue suggests that if yours is a seasonal business, you should arrange to end your year in a slack period; your accountant may suggest a date soon after 5 April because, as will be explained later, this gives you the longest period for paying your taxes.

Presenting accounts for inspection

The inspector of taxes requires to see the firm's trading account and profit and loss account, and sometimes the balance sheet (depending on the business concerned). He or she has the right (although it is seldom exercised) to ask for complete records of the whole of the firm's payments and receipts (including what has been drawn for private expenditure), supported by invoices, receipts, bank records and statements, paying-in books and cheque stubs.

If your total turnover is less than £15,000 a year you do not have to submit detailed accounts to the Inland Revenue. You must still keep accurate business records for inspection if asked, but you need only submit a simple 'three-line' account with the tax return. This gives your total turnover, total business purchases and expenses, and the resulting net profit.

It is best if the accounts are professionally drawn up by an accountant. Not only does he or she know the accepted way of presenting them, but is able to make computations of allowances and adjustments which determine, after consultation with the tax inspector, what proportion of the profits is taxable. It is in your interest to make sure that all allowances are correctly claimed; this is a complex matter, best entrusted to an expert.

Allowances on capital expenditure

Capital expenditure is money spent on plant, buildings, machinery, vehicles, and anything else that has an enduring benefit for the business and does not need to be renewed every year. It is not, in itself, tax deductible, but allowances may be given for the expenditure. In the case of a sole trader, these are currently set off against income for tax purposes; but from 1997–8, and already in the case of a limited company, they are set off against the profits.

The main allowance currently available is an annual 'writing down' allowance; but you should check with the tax office or your accountant that your intended expenditure qualifies. The benefit to you depends on the rate of allowance for the particular expenditure, the date on which it was incurred, and the timing of your claim. This can be a complicated business, and you will do well to consult your accountant when thinking of making a substantial capital purchase. The most common rate of writing down allowance is 25 per cent per annum on a reducing balance basis. This rate will normally apply to plant, equipment, furniture, fittings and motor vehicles (though any car costing over £12,000 has a separate pool with a maximum writing down allowance of £3,000 a year), but there are other rates which apply in particular circumstances.

In exceptional cases, for instance in the case of a business being started up in an enterprise zone, you may be able to claim an initial allowance instead of the writing down allowance, on the cost of constructing or acquiring a new and unused building, in the year of acquisition. This initial allowance could be as much as 100 per cent of the expenditure. Again, your accountant would be able to advise on the rates applicable to your business.

Deductible expenses

A proportion of those expenses which are not capital expenditure and which are incurred wholly and exclusively for the purposes of carrying on the business can be set off against tax. There is no definitive list of 'allowable' expenses, but items of expenditure which are generally allowed include:

- wages (including pensions, etc) of staff employed in the business (you can claim for wages paid to members of your family but only if they are genuinely employed);
- expenses of business travel (but not of going to and from home to the main place of work);
- interest on loans taken out for the acquisition or running of a business;
- interest charges on hire-purchase of capital equipment;
- hire or leasing of equipment;
- insurance premiums;
- bad debts;
- subscriptions to trade and professional associations;
- cost of self-employed retirement annuity;
- general overheads, such as telephone, heating and lighting, advertising, stationery, postage, etc;
- accountancy fees, bank charges, etc.

Bear in mind that to be tax-deductible, the wages a husband pays to his wife (or vice versa) must be commensurate with the work she or he actually does, and paid at a fair commercial rate.

If your house or telephone are used partly for your business, you may claim against tax a proportion of the expenses (rent, council tax, telephone rental, light, heating and so on). But if you claim half the council tax, say, as a business expense because, for the period of your business, only half the house is residential and the other half is commercial, then when later on you sell the house, there will be a potential capital gains tax liability on half of the appreciation in value during that time.

In the case of a car, some proportion of its cost (corresponding to the proportion of business use), may be the subject of a claim to capital allowances, and a similar proportion of the running costs may be claimed as a deductible business expense. You must, therefore, keep a record of the business mileage and the total mileage.

Tax relief for business losses

If a sole trader (or partnership) who has been in business for a number of years makes a loss, under current rules the loss can be set against any other income the trader receives in the same or the next tax year (provided he is still in the same business then). For traders starting in business from 1994–5 onwards and for existing traders from 1997–8 onwards, such a loss can be set against other income for the same or the *previous* tax year (even if he was not then in business). Under both old and new rules, if losses exceed income, the excess can be set against any capital gains for the given year.

Losses incurred in the first four years of trading may be claimed to be set against wages or other income received in the three years before the trading loss was incurred: a part of the tax paid during that period may then be refunded.

These are useful and valuable options. The sole trader can also choose to carry the losses forward to future business years to set against future profits. There would need to be special reasons to choose to do that: one reason would be that in the past he or she had not had much income and therefore had paid little or no tax. Early trading losses might then be more useful if set against future profits.

How business income tax is assessed

In the past, sole traders and partnerships have normally been taxed on a 'preceding-year basis', meaning that tax in one tax year was based on profits made in the accounting period ending in the previous tax year. But the system is being changed to a 'current-year basis', whereby tax is based on profits for the accounting period ending during the current tax year. (This is in preparation for giving everyone the option to assess their own tax bills from

1996–7 onwards.) How the new rules apply depends on whether yours is a new or an existing business.

New businesses

New businesses starting up on or after 6 April 1994 will be covered by the new system right from the start, although special rules apply to the first – and sometimes the second – tax year of your being in business:

- *first tax year* (i.e. the year in which the business' commences): tax is based on the profits from day one of trading up to 5 April. If the first accounting period ends later than 5 April, a proportion of the profits is calculated on a time basis
- *second tax year:* tax is based on the profits for the 12 months up to the end of the accounting period which ends in that tax year. If you have not been in business for a full year by then, tax is based on profits for the first 12 months including a proportion of the profits for the next accounting period. Similar adjustments are made if your first accounting period is longer than 12 months
- *third and subsequent years:* tax is based on profits for the 12 months up to the end of the accounting year which ends in that tax year.

An example will help to clarify this. Tom started trading on 6 September, fixing 5 September as his accounting year end. In his first trading year, his taxable profits were £4,800; in his second, they were £6,000; in his third, £7,000.

tax year (6–5 April)	assessment period from	to	taxable profits £
1994–5	6.9.94	5.4.95	2,800 ($\frac{7}{12}$ of 4,800)
1995–6	6.9.94	5.9.95	4,800
1996–7	6.9.95	5.9.96	6,000
1997–8	6.9.96	5.9.97	7,000

This shows that a new business's profits for the first two years are often assessed on the basis of the first 12 months of trading.

Generally speaking, therefore, the first 12 months' profits should be kept as low as possible for tax purposes.

Existing businesses

If your business is already established, you will currently be paying tax on a preceding-year basis – e.g. if you make up your accounts to end-June, your income tax bill for 1994–5 will be based on profits for the year to 30 June 1993. But you will shift on to a current-year basis according to the following timetable:

- *1994–5 and 1995–6 tax years:* taxed on preceding-year basis
- *1996–7 tax year:* transitional rules apply. For most businesses, tax will be based on the average of profits made in the accounting year ending in 1996–7 and the accounting year ending in 1995–6
- *1997–8 tax year:* taxed on current-year basis.

This means that only half the profits which you make in each of the accounting years ending in 1995–6 and 1996–7 will be taxed. In theory, it would be worthwhile ensuring that profits for those years are as high as possible. But, in practice, the Inland Revenue has announced draconian anti-tax-avoidance measures which aim to identify and penalise anyone thought to be artificially inflating their profits for those years.

When tax is payable

Under the current rules for an existing business, you pay tax in two instalments each year: on 1 January and 1 July, so tax due for 1994–5 will be paid on 1 January 1995 and 1 July 1995.

When you first start up, no assessment will, as a rule, be made until you have completed 12 months of trading; after that you are likely to receive assessments covering the tax years up to and including the current year. The tax for the first and sometimes the second year will be payable in one go, depending on when the assessments are actually made.

Once you are operating under the new current-year basis rules, tax will be due in two instalments on 31 January and 31 July. For example, tax for 1997–8 will be due on 31 January 1998 and 31 July 1998.

Even under the new rules, your choice of accounting date will affect the gap between making your profits and paying tax on them. Tom makes his first tax payment barely five months after the end of his trading year. If his accounting date were 31 April, the payment would not be due until nine months after his year-end.

Changes to sole traders and partnerships

If a sole trader decides to take a partner, or a partnership takes an additional partner (or partners) or loses one or more, then for income tax purposes the business is usually deemed to have stopped trading when the old arrangement ended, and to have started trading again when the new arrangement started.

However, this need not happen for tax purposes if all partners, both before and after the change, request the tax inspector, within two years of the change, to treat the trading as continuing.

Corporation tax: limited companies

Most of what has been said about income tax on business profits (also known as Schedule D income tax) applies to the payment of corporation tax. Here are the main differences between the two.

Corporation tax is the tax which companies pay on their profits. There are two different rates:

- a full rate – 33 per cent in 1994–5
- a small-company rate – 25 per cent in 1994–5.

A small company is currently defined as one whose annual profits are £300,000 or less: up to this amount, the lower tax rate of 25 per cent is charged on all profits. Above this, the rate of tax gradually increases, according to a simple formula, until at £1,500,000 the full rate of 33 per cent applies, on all profits.

How not to pay corporation tax

One material difference between a sole trader and a company lies in the fact that the salaries paid to company directors are a business cost, like any other salaries, and so are deducted in calculating profits. As the directors' remuneration need not be fixed until the results of the year's trading are known, it may be advantageous to a small company to pay out all its trading surplus as directors' salaries, on which they pay individual income tax. (For the remuneration to qualify as a deduction, however, the company must be able to show that it was paid or was made available 'wholly and exclusively for the purpose of the trade'.) Any part of the surplus that is not paid out is known as 'retained profit' and is subjected to corporation tax.

Your accountant will advise you how to apportion your profits between salaries and retained profits to your best advantage. He or she will also be needed for drawing up the accounts because, although corporation tax returns are not particularly complicated, the Companies Act 1985 demands more advanced and complex accounting from a company than is the case for a sole trader. This Act also requires that company accounts be audited by a suitably qualified accountant. However, from mid-1994 companies with a turnover of no more than £90,000 a year will be exempt from this requirement. Companies with a turnover above that limit but less than £350,000 a year (and a balance sheet of no more than £1.4 million) will be allowed to submit a less rigorous report from an independent accountant.

Capital allowances and losses: limited company

These are the same for companies as for sole traders and partnerships, but cannot be offset against the directors' or shareholders' income from other sources: they apply only to the company's income.

A trading loss in any one period may be offset, retrospectively, against the profits in the previous three years; claims must be made within two years. (Losses in accounting periods ending before 1 April 1991 can be carried back against the previous year's profit only.) Or else the loss may be carried forward to offset the profits of subsequent years; the period in which losses may be carried forward is indefinite but the claims must be made within six years.

Losses may only be carried forward to offset the profit from the same trade in subsequent years.

Accounting period: limited company

A company may choose any date it likes for its accounting period. Corporation tax is, however, charged by reference to the fiscal financial year which runs from 1 April to 31 March and if (as is often the case) the company's accounting period is different, then the trading profits of two periods will be apportioned on a time basis. For instance, if a company has chosen January to December as its accounting period, then the apportionment will take 9/12 of trading profits of one period and 3/12 of the other one. Other income and any capital gains are not apportioned; their actual date decides which fiscal financial year they come into.

Tax is due nine months from the end of the accounting period (that is, September in the case of a January to December accounting period).

Capital profits

Sole traders and partnerships, as well as limited companies, from time to time make capital profits: for example, on the sale of a business property or goodwill. Sole traders and partners may be liable to capital gains tax on the capital profit; limited companies do not pay capital gains tax, but instead pay corporation tax on capital profit calculated in accordance with the capital gains tax regulations.

The calculations of any tax liability on the disposal of a business asset and of the reliefs available are very complex, and professional assistance from your accountant will almost certainly be necessary.

The main reliefs available against capital gains are as follows:

- *indexation allowance:* this deducts any gains due to inflation since March 1982. But from 6 April 1995 onwards indexation allowances may not be used to create or increase a capital loss, and in the meantime such losses are restricted
- *capital losses:* these can be set against gains
- *tax-free allowance:* individuals (e.g. sole traders) can make gains up to a given amount each year tax-free
- *re-investment relief:* from 30 November 1993 onwards, tax due on any gains made by individuals – but not companies – may

be deferred if the proceeds are re-invested in the shares of an unquoted trading company, provided certain conditions are met

- *retirement relief:* where an individual disposes of a business or certain assets on retirement, the first £250,000 of any gain is tax-free together with half the next £750,000 of gain. This relief is scaled down if you have been running the business for less than ten years
- *hold-over relief:* if you give away business assets or shares in an unquoted company – e.g. by passing them on to younger members of your family – you may be able to defer any CGT that would otherwise be due.

Value Added Tax (VAT)

This is a tax normally payable quarterly, not to the Inland Revenue but to HM Customs and Excise, on the supply of most goods and services in Great Britain. It consists of input and output tax. There are three kinds of registration: compulsory, voluntary and intending.

The tax you pay on goods and services that you buy for your business is called *input tax*: the tax you charge your customers is called *output tax*. At present, the main rate for both is 17.5 per cent.

This is how it works: Bill buys raw materials for £235, inclusive of 17.5 per cent VAT; £35 is his input tax. He uses the materials to manufacture products selling for £450, before VAT. So the selling price would amount to £528.75 of which £78.75 is his output tax. He deducts the input tax from it, and remits the balance (£43.75) to Customs and Excise. If his input tax had been greater than his output tax, he would have been refunded the difference.

At present there are four categories of goods and services:

- *exempt:* on which no VAT is payable under any circumstances (for example, insurance, doctors' services)
- *zero-rated:* on which, in theory, tax is payable but, in practice, none is paid, because the tax rate is zero per cent (for example, exported goods and food in shops)

- *standard-rated:* on which VAT at 17.5 per cent is charged. This applies to the majority of goods and services. The figure is liable to change at the Government's decision.
- *reduced-rated:* domestic fuel on which VAT is charged at 8 per cent for 1994–5 but due to rise to the full 17.5 per cent from April 1995.

The difference between exempt and zero-rated may seem trivial, but is actually important. You cannot claim refunds of input tax unless you are collecting output tax, if only notionally. If you dealt only in exempt supplies, you would not be a 'taxable person', and could not be registered for VAT. You could not then recover any of the input tax you paid on your supplies, such as telephone charges and stationery, any more than a private person can.

However, this is not the case if you deal only in zero-rated supplies (for example, if you are an exporter). You can claim refunds of your input tax – unless you exercise a zero-rated option of trader's exemption from VAT, in which case you lose these refunds.

Compulsory registration

You must register for VAT if, at the end of any month, your total taxable turnover exceeds £45,000 or if you have reasonable grounds for believing that your taxable turnover in the next 30 days will exceed £45,000.

Trade in zero-rated supplies counts towards your turnover, but not trade in exempt supplies.

If you buy a going concern from a VAT-registered trader, you must be registered too – and may be allowed to go on using the same VAT registration number, although this should only be considered after careful discussion with your accountant or solicitor, since it would make you liable for amounts owed to Customs and Excise by the previous business. (If you decide VAT registration is not to your advantage, perhaps if you intend to run the business on a smaller scale, you can apply for deregistration.) You should get your registration in order before you sign the contract to buy the business. There is a leaflet (700/9/85) available from your VAT office, about buying a going concern.

As soon as you know that you will have to register for VAT, contact your local VAT office, at Customs and Excise, who will send you forms to fill in. Once you have done this, you must immediately start charging your customers VAT and keeping records, without waiting to be allotted a registration number because you yourself will be charged VAT from the moment you become liable for registration. However, you must not show VAT as a separate item in your invoices until you have been allocated a VAT registration number. Include the amount of the tax in your prices, and tell your customers that you have done so. Then, within 30 days of getting your registration number, you must send out another set of invoices, showing VAT separately, to those of your customers who will be claiming it back, being themselves registered.

It is best not to get into arrears, which you may find it difficult to recover from your customers in retrospect. And it is worth setting up a system from the very beginning, because it is hard to do several months' books in arrears.

You must keep records of all transactions: do not make guesses. Keep for inspection all invoices you receive which show payment of VAT. You have to make quarterly returns showing your input and output tax, and to submit to having your VAT records inspected at intervals. There are civil penalties for defaulting on payments, or for failing to register for VAT on time.

VAT leaflet CE 700/1, *Should I Be Registered for VAT?* explains in detail the compulsory registration rules.

Voluntary registration

With a turnover under £45,000 a year, you may still apply for registration if you are able to convince Customs and Excise that this is applicable to your business. Some of the advantages of registration are:

- You can claim back all your input tax (for instance, on equipment you have to buy when setting up). This is especially advantageous if your goods or services are zero-rated.
- If you start trading unregistered and your turnover grows to the point where you have to register, the addition of VAT will

increase all your prices: this will dismay your customers, if they are consumers and not registered traders, and so cannot claim back the increase.

- VAT can ease your cash flow difficulties. If you arrange to make major purchases just before you are due to make out a return, your input VAT will be refunded shortly after you get the invoice, even though you may be receiving 3 months' credit from your suppliers. (But this scheme will work against you if you yourself give credit to customers: you will have to pay your output VAT months before you yourself get paid.)

Some of the disadvantages of registration are:

- The record-keeping and accounting demanded by VAT are an addition to your labours which you may not welcome if you employ a small number of staff, or none. Matters become still more complicated if you deal in a variety of goods, some standard-rated and others zero-rated, for example, stationery and books.
- If you are an exporter, you must be able to prove (by means of the relevant shipping documents) that your goods were, in fact, sold abroad. If some of your trade is in export and some is home trade, you will have the complication of selling goods differently rated.

Intending trader registration

If you are starting a business in the course of which you intend to produce 'taxable supplies' at some future date, but have not yet started to do so, you can apply for VAT registration beforehand. You will have to show convincing documentary evidence (such as contracts, licences, planning permission) of firm arrangements to make the taxable supplies. If this is accepted, you may be able to claim back some of the input tax you yourself have paid, provided that it is wholly attributable to the intended production of taxable supplies.

Cash accounting scheme

This is open to all firms whose taxable turnover (excluding VAT) does not exceed £300,000. Under this scheme, VAT accounts are rendered, not on the basis of the tax invoices, but on the basis of money actually paid and received. This offers special advantages to businesses giving extended credit to customers – they need not account for VAT on credit transactions until they have received payment, and they enjoy automatic bad debt relief.

This scheme is not particularly advantageous, however, to traders, such as most retailers, who are paid in full at the time of the sale.

Retail schemes

Customs and Excise provides a number of retail schemes for calculating VAT: these are intended for shopkeepers and other retail traders, for whom the system of issuing a tax invoice for each sale would be impracticable. There is a choice of some 10 retail schemes, of which one or more could be appropriate; consult your VAT office before deciding on any of them.

Annual accounting scheme

This is open to traders who have already been registered for at least one year, and whose annual taxable turnover (excluding VAT) does not exceed £300,000. It works like this: your VAT liability is estimated on the basis of the previous year's payments, and divided into ten monthly portions. Nine of these you pay by direct debit, starting at the end of the fourth month of your accounting year. You then have two months for sending in your annual VAT return, and making the tenth, balancing payment.

This system means that you have to make only one return a year, instead of four; and knowing in advance how much you are going to be paying, you are spared unpleasant jolts to your cash-flow calculations. The balancing payment is less predictable, but you have an extra month's grace.

CHAPTER 8

HOW TO BE AN EMPLOYER

YES, THERE is such a thing as a one-man or one-woman business, particularly if what is being offered is a service or a consultancy. A plumber or electrician, for instance, needs only a telephone-answering machine to record customers' calls: he or she can call them back in the evenings, and do the bookkeeping on Sundays.

Many small firms start up with no other staff than the entrepreneur and his or her family, or a partner. But unless the family is large and willing, the firm will soon be needing some other employees, if it is to achieve progress.

In fact, a manufacturing business is likely to need employees from the start. It may only be a case of a couple of part-timers, or outworkers, or one trained secretary; even so, the businessman or businesswoman immediately becomes an employer, and should find out how to go about it.

Finding and recruiting staff

When you have decided to take on employees, start by defining exactly what their duties are to be and what experience, skills and qualities are required to do the job. Avoid the temptation to ask for experience and qualifications greater than are necessary. This will make it easier for you to find the right person and easier, also, for any applicant to decide whether the job is the right one for him or her. A good working relationship is much more likely to develop if both you and your workers are well suited to each other.

Ways of finding suitable employees include the Employment Service (listed in the telephone directory), employment agencies (which charge the employer a fee), personal recommendation or advertisements in your local or national or trade press or local radio stations.

If you have a shop or factory with an entrance on the main road, place an advertisement where it can be seen by passers-by. Or advertise for new workers by placing cards in local shops. This is cheap and generally produces a good response. Specify exactly what is wanted – and if you are willing to train new staff, make this clear.

It is sometimes easier and more economical to contract casual, part-time or freelance workers than employ full-time permanent staff, particularly when employing people with family commitments who are keen to get jobs which can be done partly at home, or with flexible hours, perhaps not coming in to work during school holidays.

It can be a bad mistake to employ acquaintances; this can prove embarrassing if they turn out to be no good. Also, do not try to recruit staff when you already have large orders and are very busy. This would be inefficient because it does not allow time for training.

Remember that any advertisement, wherever it is placed, must not exclude anyone on grounds of race or sex, except in a very few closely defined cases.

Your local Employment Service can provide a fast, free recruitment service for all types of jobs, and staff can advise on selection and can provide information on employment legislation.

You may decide to employ young people and train them yourself: the Government offers some financial incentives to firms willing to help reduce unemployment among school-leavers. Consult your local careers service office about this and for advice on training.

If you are looking for a worker with a particular skill which is in short supply locally, your local Employment Service can give a wide circulation to the vacancy, to attract workers from other areas.

Workers with particular skills may already be employed elsewhere and you may need to offer them terms that are in some way an improvement on what they are getting or can get in their present jobs. If a worker is at present employed locally, make sure his or her existing contract of employment does not prohibit him or her from leaving to take up a similar job within, say, five miles of the existing workplace, otherwise both of you could end up with a costly court case.

If you ask for references, be sure to take them up, preferably in writing.

Paying wages and salaries

A factor affecting wage levels may be an agreement between the employers' federation of your trade and the appropriate trade unions, which may be binding on you. If there are similar businesses in the area, it is wise to find out what they are paying, and if it is related to a union rate. Men and women doing the same or broadly similar work are, of course, entitled to the same rates of pay.

Your accountant will tell you how to set up a wages book, and may even agree, for a fee, to look after your payroll until you are sufficiently organised to take care of it yourself.

Avoiding employment disputes

The independent Advisory, Conciliation and Arbitration Service (ACAS) can be consulted on matters relating to employment and industrial relations. Though this organisation is mostly known to the public as a conciliator in industrial disputes or disputes between individuals and their employers, a considerable part of its work is preventive and consists of advising both sides of industry on industrial relations matters, including finding their way through the complications of employment legislation.

The ACAS head office is at 27 Wilton Street, London SW1X 7AZ   TEL 071-388 5100: offices in Scotland, Wales and in the English regions deal with written and telephone enquiries. Their addresses and telephone numbers can be found in local telephone directories. Visits to employers' premises by ACAS advisers can be arranged, and free booklets are available about recruitment and selection, workplace communications, job evaluation, discipline at work, and other aspects of employment.

Rights of employees

It is important for new entrepreneurs to understand the rights of employees under current legislation. ACAS has produced three codes of practice (obtainable from HMSO): *Disciplinary Practice and Procedures in Employment*; *Disclosure of Information to Trade Unions for Collective Bargaining Purposes*; and *Time Off for Trade Union Duties and Activities*.

It has also produced a free booklet, entitled *Employing People*, specially for small firms; it contains straightforward guidance on a wide range of employment matters, from hiring people and employment contracts, to absence, labour turnover and unfair dismissal. In addition, the Department of Employment publishes booklets on employment legislation which cover every topic that you should be informed about. You can get copies from your local Employment Service office. Only a brief outline can be given here.

The 1978 Employment Protection (Consolidation) Act makes a distinction between full-time and part-time employee. Employees working 16 hours or more a week count as full-time and are entitled to a range of workplace rights after two years with the same employer. Part-timers, working between eight and 16 hours a week, have to wait five years before getting the same rights. In March 1994, the House of Lords ruled that this distinction is against European Union law, therefore, with immediate effect, part-timers must be given the same rights as full-time employees.

Written statement of main terms and conditions of employment (PL700)

You must give every employee a written statement setting out the conditions and terms on which he or she is employed (sometimes called a 'contract of employment', though that is not strictly correct: the contract was formed earlier, when you made someone a firm offer of a job and it was firmly accepted. This is legally enforceable as soon as an employee starts work.)

The written statement must be given within 13 weeks of starting work and contain information on at least these points:

- name of the employer and employee
- whether employment with a previous employer counts as part of continuous period of employment
- date of starting employment
- title of job or description of employee's job
- rates of pay (including overtime, if any) and how they are calculated
- whether payment is to be by cheque, cash or bank transfer
- when payment is to be made (weekly or monthly)
- hours of work (regular and overtime, if applicable)
- public holidays and holiday pay
- sick pay arrangements
- pension scheme arrangements (including whether there is a pension scheme contracted out of the State Earnings-Related Pensions Scheme)
- length of notice required from employer and from employee
- rules relating to disciplinary procedures, such as warnings and dismissal, and procedure for taking up grievances
- length of employment – if not permanent
- place of work
- collective agreements
- rules relating to requirements to work outside the UK.

If any of these points does not apply, for instance if there are no pension arrangements, the document must say so explicitly.

It is the practice of many employers to confirm an oral offer of job by a letter, setting out the conditions and terms. If all these above points are covered, such a letter will do in place of a written statement; if they are not, a written statement will still be necessary.

The terms set out in the statement cannot be altered without the consent of both parties. If you transfer the employee to another kind of work or promote him or her, you may need to provide a new written statement.

Itemised pay statements (PL704)
With each wage payment, you must give each employee a wage slip showing gross pay, deductions (with the reason given for

each, such as income tax, National Insurance contributions, union dues), and the net pay.

You will, of course, need to keep a copy of this for your own records. If you pay wages in cash, get your copy signed by the employee, as a receipt.

Guarantee payments (PL724)
If business is bad, you may want to put some employees on short time, or even lay them off without pay, or with pay at a lower rate. Your right to do so should be specified at the time of engaging an employee. You should also be aware that most employees are entitled to a guaranteed payment for up to five working days in any three months in which you have no work for them to do.

Continuous employment (PL711)
Many employees' rights depend on their being continuously employed. Some breaks in employment, such as maternity leave, don't break continuity; others, no matter how short, do. The full rules are explained in the leaflet.

Time off for public duties (PL702)
You should allow time off (sometimes with pay) to employees engaged on public duties: for example, justices of the peace, local councillors, school managers or governors, trade union officials.

Maternity entitlements (PL710)
A pregnant employee has the right to time off without loss of pay for visits to antenatal clinics. Where an employee is stopping work to have a baby, she may be entitled to statutory maternity pay (SMP). These are the qualifying conditions:

- she must have been working for you continuously for at least 26 weeks continuing into the 15th week before the baby is due (this fifteenth week is known as the qualifying week)
- she must have average weekly earnings of not less than the current lower earnings limit for the payment of National Insurance contributions
- she must still be pregnant in the 11th week before the expected week of confinement, or must have already given birth (there are special regulations for premature births)
- she must have stopped working for you.

A woman fulfilling these conditions can get SMP for 18 weeks during a period which starts not earlier than the 11th week before the expected date of confinement. If you count as a 'small employer' (paying £20,000 a year or less in gross National Insurance contributions), you may deduct the gross amount of the SMP from the total sum of National Insurance contributions (your own and your staff's) which you have to forward to the Inland Revenue's Collector of Taxes. From September 1994, larger employers may reclaim only 92 per cent of the SMP payments. You may also deduct a proportion of the employer's part of the National Insurance contribution paid by you on the SMP.

If your employee has worked for you for at least two years, she is entitled to come back to work for you in her former job (or a suitable alternative where it is not reasonably practical for you to offer her the former job) at any time up to the end of the 29th week after the birth of the child. But she must tell you of her intention to return to work (in writing, at least 21 days before her absence begins) and must produce a certificate (MATB1) of expected confinement, if you want to see it. Not earlier than 49 days after the expected confinement, you may write to ask her if she still intends to return, and she must reply within 14 days. She must also let you know the date on which she wants to return, at least 21 days in advance.

If you have no more than five employees when a woman starts her maternity leave, you may not have to keep her job open for her.

When employees fall ill

Under the statutory sick pay scheme (SSP), an employer must pay employees sick pay for up to 28 weeks' illness. Spells of illness shorter than four days (including Saturdays, Sundays and holidays) do not qualify for sick pay. The 28-week maximum 'period of incapacity for work' is not limited to one tax year: it may be made up of intermittent periods of illness, provided that the gap between any of these is not more than eight weeks. When an employee's illness, whether 'linked' or continuous, lasts longer than 28 weeks, your obligation ceases and state benefit takes over; but your obligation starts again if, having recovered, the employee should fall ill again more than eight weeks after the end of a maximum period.

If you count as a 'small employer' (paying £20,000 a year or less in gross National Insurance contributions), you can recover what you pay in SSP by deducting it from that month's total of National Insurance contributions, before forwarding the balance to the Inland Revenue. Larger employers cannot reclaim any of the SSP they pay.

For a detailed explanation of these rules, and also those of maternity entitlements, consult the Social Security booklets NI270, *SSP Manual* and NI257, *SMP Manual* available from your Social Security office.

The Department of Social Security has a free telephone service giving advice to employers about statutory sick pay, statutory maternity pay, and National Insurance contributions. This service is intended to be particularly helpful to new or established small businesses without a separate wages department. The number is (0800) 393539.

Disciplinary procedures

Disciplinary procedures can help to ensure that disciplinary offences are dealt with fairly and consistently, as well as minimising disagreements about disciplinary matters and reducing the need for dismissals. This may be particularly important if an employee should complain to an industrial tribunal of unfair dismissal, since the employer will need to show the tribunal that the dismissal was fair.

Disciplinary rules
Clear rules benefit both employer and employees, set standards of conduct at work, and make clear to employees what is expected of them. Employees will more readily accept rules if care is taken to explain why they are necessary. Rules should cover such matters as timekeeping; absence; health and safety; use of company telephones, equipment and other facilities; and race and sex discrimination.

The rules should also specify the kind of offences that will be regarded as gross misconduct, and which could lead to dismissal without notice. Serious offences such as physical violence, theft or fraud are normally so regarded, but the nature of the business or other circumstances may determine that other offences should also be included.

The ACAS code of practice

The ACAS Code, *Disciplinary Practice and Procedure in Employment*, recommends that disciplinary procedures should:

- be in writing
- specify to whom they apply
- provide for matters to be dealt with quickly
- indicate the disciplinary actions which may be taken
- specify the levels of management which have the authority to take the various forms of disciplinary action, ensuring that immediate superiors do not normally have the power to dismiss without reference to senior management
- provide for individuals to be informed of the complaints against them, and to be given an opportunity to state their case before decisions are reached
- give individuals the right to be accompanied by a trade union representative, or by a fellow employee of their choice when stating their case
- ensure that, except for gross misconduct, no employees are dismissed for a first breach of discipline
- ensure that disciplinary action is not taken until the case has been carefully investigated
- ensure that individuals are given an explanation for any penalty imposed
- provide a right to appeal and specify the procedure to be followed.

In addition, disciplinary procedures should:

- apply to all employees, irrespective of their length of service
- be non-discriminatory, and applied irrespective of sex, marital status or race
- ensure that any investigatory period of suspension is with pay, and specify how pay is to be calculated during such a period (if, exceptionally, suspension is to be without pay, this should be provided for in the contract of employment)

- ensure that, where the facts are in dispute, no disciplinary penalty is imposed until the case has been carefully investigated and it has been concluded, on the balance of probability, that the employee committed the act in question.

Disciplinary penalties

Informal action, such as counselling, should generally precede formal warnings. If an informal approach fails, then formal penalties are normally implemented progressively. There are typically four stages:

- oral warning
- first written warning
- final written warning
- dismissal.

While there are normally three stages before dismissal, they may be dispensed with if the employee's alleged misconduct warrants such action.

Rights to notice

An employee who has worked for you for four weeks or more is entitled to a week's notice or a week's salary in lieu of notice, unless the contract of employment specified a longer period of notice. After two years, one week's notice is required for each year of working for you, up to a maximum of 12 weeks. Every employee is entitled to a written statement of the reason for being dismissed, if he or she asks for one.

The ACAS advisory handbook *Discipline at Work* contains comprehensive practical advice on handling disciplinary matters, and gives examples of rules, and of a disciplinary procedure for a small company.

Industrial tribunal

A dismissed employee may bring a complaint of unfair dismissal to an industrial tribunal only after a minimum of two years' continuous employment. However, there is no qualifying period for employees who allege that they were dismissed because of trade union activity, or because of sex or race discrimination.

The industrial tribunal will take account of the firm's size and resources when deciding whether a dismissal was fair or not, and whether to direct re-employment. For instance, if a worker has proved not up to the physical demands of the job, a small firm may not have another job to offer, and may therefore dismiss the employee.

Consult *Rights to Notice and Reasons for Dismissal* (PL707). Other useful publications from the Department of Employment are: *Fair and Unfair Dismissal: a guide for employers* (PL714) and *The Law on Unfair Dismissal: guidance for small firms* (PL715).

Making employees redundant

Employees may have to be made redundant when a firm is not doing enough business to justify their employment. A redundancy dismissal can be unfair on the basis of improper selection, lack of consultation and lack of notice. It should certainly not be motivated by personal reasons. A worker who thinks you are making him redundant just to get rid of him or her can challenge your decision before an industrial tribunal.

Redundancy pay is due to those employees who have at least two years' continuous service. Service before the age of 18 does not count. See *Redundancy Payments* (PL808).

There is an obligation on the employer to inform the local Department of Employment if he or she is going to make ten or more people redundant. You will find the address of your local office in the telephone directory. Look also at *Redundancy Consultation and Notification* (PL833).

An employee with two years' continuous employment who is being made redundant is entitled to time off with pay to look for or to train for other work. Consult *Facing Redundancy? Time Off for Job Hunting* (PL703).

If the employees are members of a trade union, there is an obligation for the employer to consult with the trade union at the 'earliest opportunity'. Where ten or more redundancies are proposed within a 30-day period, then the employers are required to enter into at least 30 days' consultation with the trade union before the first dismissal takes place; where more than 100 redundancies are proposed within a 90-day period, then at least 90 days' consultation is required before the first dismissal takes place.

One important point to be aware of if you take over a going concern, is that workers' employment is deemed in law to be continuing. So if you decide to replace some of them, you may find yourself with a good deal of compensation to pay, even though you did not hire these people, and they have not worked for you for very long. This is one of the dangers of taking over a going concern, so before you do so, ask for a roll of employees, showing their length of continuous employment there, so that you can assess the amount of possible redundancy pay.

Look also at *Employment Rights on Transferring an Undertaking* (PL699). If you know in advance that you will want to make employees redundant, negotiate with the seller of the business about which of you is to pay.

Other points to bear in mind

If any of your employees are members of a trade union, you will do well to read *Union Membership and Non-membership Rights* (PL871) and *Industrial Action and the Law* (PL870). Note also that a trade union official may legitimately ask for time off for his or her duties: this is covered by an ACAS code of practice.

You should also be aware that there are laws concerning sex and race discrimination in employment. The Equal Opportunities Commission, Overseas House, Quay Street, Manchester M3 3HN TEL 061-833 9244, publishes leaflets and booklets on sex discrimination; for information on the Race Relations Act contact the Commission for Racial Equality, Elliot House, 10/12 Allington Street, London SW1E 5EH TEL 071-828 7022.

A two-day course on employment law is amongst the courses organised by The Industrial Society, Robert Hyde House, 48 Bryanston Square, London W1H 7LN TEL 071-262 2401.

Health and safety of employees

The responsibilities concerning the health, safety and welfare of people at work are defined in broad terms by the Health and Safety at Work etc Act 1974. It places important general duties on all people at work – employers, employees and the self-employed, manufacturers, suppliers, designers and importers of materials used at work, and people in control of premises. More detailed and specific requirements for particular kinds of work are laid down by other legislation, such as the Offices Shops and Railways Premises Act 1963 which specifies what must be provided in the way of washrooms, lavatories, heat, ventilation and light, somewhere to sit, and so on. The Factories Act 1961 and other statutes and regulations apply to many different work activities.

The requirements to protect health and safety and provide welfare vary considerably depending on the type of work being carried on. You will need to find out how your business will be affected and what facilities and safeguards you must provide in matters such as machinery guards, protective clothing, storage and handling of dangerous substances.

If in doubt, consult the appropriate enforcing authority – who may come to inspect your premises. Generally, the enforcing authority is the local authority for most shops, offices, hotel and catering activities. For other businesses, it is the Health and Safety Executive, whose factory inspectorate must be notified of any premises to be used as a factory, at least one month beforehand.

Addresses of local authority enforcement offices can be obtained from district council offices or, in case of difficulty, from the local authority liaison officer in the nearest HSE area office. There are some 20 such offices, and an enquiry point at Broad Lane, Sheffield S3 7HQ   TEL (0742) 892345.

The HSE publishes a range of explanatory and guidance material; some publications are available free of charge from HSE offices. The booklet, *A Guide to the HSW Act* (HS)(R)(6), is obtainable from HMSO or bookshops. The HSE produces a list of all its publications, and this is available free of charge from the enquiry point (see above) or its leaflet line on (0742) 892346. There are also free subject catalogues covering topics such as agriculture, asbestos, construction work.

All accidents at work must be recorded and all serious ones, which lead to having three or more days off or at least one day in hospital, must be reported on a special form to the local Health and Safety Executive. Near-miss accidents must also be reported.

Every place of work should have a well-equipped first-aid box (equipped according to the number of employees on site), the contents of which are specified. The employees should know where it is kept and there should be a correct ratio of trained first-aiders to staff (in offices it is 1:150).

PAYE

You are the channel by which your employees' Paye As You Earn (PAYE) income tax is transmitted to the Board of Inland Revenue, as well as their NI contributions (and yours, too).

Leaflet IR53, *Thinking of Taking Someone On?*, obtainable from the Inspector of Taxes and from PAYE enquiry offices, explains and clearly illustrates the procedure.

If you employ anyone in your business in return for wages, even members of your own family, you are responsible for deducting their income tax and National Insurance at source and sending it to the Inland Revenue. (As a small employer you can pay quarterly rather than monthly.) As soon as you hire someone, let your tax office know: you will be told which is to be your PAYE office. You will then be told what your employee's PAYE reference number will be, and shortly after that you will receive a copy of the 'New Employer's Starter Pack'. Included in the pack is a copy of *Employer's Guide to PAYE*, which covers the main points of the system, together with detailed information about particular cases.

An employee who has previously been employed and paid tax should bring you his or her P45 form which has on it a code number and total pay and total tax to date in the financial year. A new employee who has not paid PAYE tax before, must be given form P46 which you can get from the Inland Revenue office, and an emergency code number.

The tax inspector will send you two sets of printed tables, *Free pay table A*, and *PAYE taxable pay tables B–D*. By looking up each code number in the tables, you will know how much tax to deduct each week or month. You enter the amount, the gross salary and other details on each employee's deductions working sheet, which has a space for each week of the tax year. At regular intervals you must send the deducted tax and insurance contributions to the Collector of Taxes.

At the end of the tax year, all the information concerning each employee's wages, income tax and National Insurance contributions must be entered on a triplicate form P14. Two copies are sent to the PAYE tax district, together with forms P35: *Employer's Annual Statement, Declaration and Certificate*. The third (certificate P60) goes to the employee.

National Insurance

As an employer, you are also responsible for collecting all your employees' National Insurance contributions every week or month, together with their income tax, and sending them on to the Inland Revenue together with yours, the employer's contributions. You work out the contributions from tables supplied by the Inland Revenue.

Arrangements exist for employees to contract out of part of their contributions where a firm has an occupational pension scheme, but this is unlikely to concern you at this stage.

You will be concerned with three kinds of contributions, as listed:

National Insurance contributions (as from April 1994)

Type of contribution	Category of insured person	Basis of contribution	Earnings limits lower	upper	Amount paid
Class 1	employed earners	earnings-related	£57.00 a week	£430 a week (employees only)	employee: nil if you earn less than £57; otherwise, 2% on first £57 and 10% on the rest up to £430 employer: nil if earnings less than £57; otherwise, up to 10.2%
Class 2	self-employed	flat rate	—	—	£5.65 a week
Class 4	self-employed	earnings-related	£6,490	£22,360 annual profits	7.3% of amount by which profits exceed lower limit, up to £22,360

Class 1 contributions

These are due from each of your employees who is sixteen or over and below the minimum pension age (65 for a man, 60 for a woman) whose earnings reach the lower earnings limit. For each of them, you must pay the employer's share. (Contributions are not due from employees over pension age, but you must continue to pay the employer's share.) Obviously the lower earnings limit figure is one to bear in mind when employing part-time staff. If you go over this limit, both the employee and you have to pay National Insurance contributions, and an apparently generous pay increase may prove a lot less lavish after extra deductions for National Insurance and tax.

If yours is a limited company, you as an individual pay an employee's share, and the company pays the employer's contribution – although, in effect, in a small company you would be paying both the sums.

Class 2 contributions

You pay these if you are a sole trader or a partner, and there are some benefits from which you are excluded, notably unemployment benefit. You can claim exemption from class 2 payments if you are able to show that your net earnings from self-employment in a tax year are expected to be below a certain sum. You must apply to the Department of Social Security for a certificate of exemption in advance. The certificate cannot normally be back-calculated, and any contributions already paid cannot be refunded.

If you start your business in your spare time while continuing to work for an employer, you must pay both class 1 and class 2 contributions. There is, however, an upper limit, and anything you pay over this amount in a tax year will be refunded to you. It is no longer possible to buy National Insurance stamps. You pay either by quarterly bills or monthly direct debit.

Class 4 contributions

These are payable by class 2 payers whose taxable profits exceed a certain sum; there is an upper limit on the amount payable.

Class 4 contributions are assessed together with income tax by the Inland Revenue and are collected at the same time as your income tax (Schedule D). If you expect your contributions to go over the set limits in any year, you can apply to defer the payment till your earnings have been assessed for tax. Fifty per cent of your class 4 contributions may be offset against your business profits in calculating your tax liability.

For fuller information about National Insurance, go directly to the source, the Department of Social Security. Annually updated leaflets include the following:

NP28	*National Insurance Contributions for Employees*
NI35	*National Insurance for Company Directors*
NI268	*National Insurance: Quick Guide for Employers*
NI269	*Employer's Manual on National Insurance Contributions*
NI270	*Statutory Sick Pay Manual for Employers*
NI278	*Statutory Sick Pay Small Employers' Relief*
NI257	*Statutory Maternity Pay Manual for Employers*
NP18	*National Insurance Contributions for Self-employed People*
NI27A	*National Insurance Contributions for Self-employed People with Small Earnings*
NI255	*National Insurance Contributions: Direct Debit*

CHAPTER 9

INSURANCE FOR THE SMALL BUSINESS

WHEN YOU are just starting up in business and every penny counts, having to pay insurance premiums can seem to be an uncalled-for imposition. But you would see this in a different light if the occasion arose to put in a claim. Then you might start to worry whether you had taken enough insurance to cover all the losses you had suffered.

Insurance is best thought of as the price of peace of mind. Accidents will happen, as everyone knows. Make sure, if you take out insurance, that the cover is adequate – otherwise, you might as well not bother.

Almost every aspect of trading can create a need for some kind of insurance. For most kinds you can find cover, but sometimes the premium may be high.

The premiums paid for any business insurance are deductible expenses which can be set off against tax.

Employer's liability insurance

The law requires that everyone on your payroll (except for members of your family and domestic servants) must be covered by this insurance, and that a current certificate of insurance be displayed at the place of work.

The employer's liability insurance covers you for claims that might arise if an employee suffered physical injury or illness in the course of, or resulting from, his or her employment. This could be anything from a twisted ankle after falling down stairs to losing a limb. It would be necessary for the employee suing you for damages to show that the injury or illness arose not from his or her own inadvertence, but from your negligence or that of another employee.

You would be wise to include employed members of the family in the insurance cover, even though you do not need to. Close relationship does not preclude a claim for damages, and if one of your nearest and dearest were to suffer, you would be glad to have him or her compensated by the insurance company.

Most insurance companies will quote you rates for this type of insurance. The premiums are related to the size of your payroll and will also depend on the risks attached to the jobs. If your employees do office work only, it is likely to cost less than if they work with machinery or shift heavy loads.

The Health and Safety Executive publishes a brochure, *Short Guide to the Employer's Liability (Compulsory Insurance) Act 1969* (HSE 4), which is available free on request from the address on page 93.

Material damage insurance

You would be foolhardy not to insure for the various disasters that could mean the rapid end of your business, such as burglary, fire, flood, subsidence, malicious damage, explosion, to name but a few. Some of the features of a business that should be covered are:

- the business premises (including site clearance and rebuilding costs)
- the contents (including fixtures and fittings, industrial plant, tools and other equipment)
- the stock (including supplies not yet used and goods that have been allocated to customers, even if the customer has not yet paid for them)
- goods in transit (on the way to the customer, or to a sub-contractor, or to the docks for shipment; in your own or someone else's vehicles; sent by post)
- goods on a sub-contractor's premises.

You could take out a separate policy for each kind of risk, but it would be more efficient to have a single material damage insurance policy covering all risks.

Many trade associations arrange (or act as agents for) special insurance policies tailored for the needs of the particular trade.

The insurance should be revised and updated at regular intervals, otherwise you might find a huge discrepancy between the amount you are covered for and what your loss actually amounts to, if you need to make a claim.

Consequential loss insurance

This is a corollary to material damage insurance: it covers further losses which would arise if your business were to come to a standstill following a disaster that is covered by the insurance. Should your premises burn down, for instance, you would not only need to rebuild and re-equip but would also have to pay your wage bill and some overheads costs while no money was coming in. You might have lost all your stock and your office records and files, and by the time you were back in business, your customers might have gone elsewhere.

Consequential loss insurance should cover all these situations, loss of profit, and your overheads costs for a limited period (known as the indemnity period). Usually this is not less than 12 months; you may be able to negotiate a longer period, and the particular features of your business may need other special terms.

Public liability insurance

Apart from the statutory insurance for liability to employees, there is insurance to cover you for claims by members of the public who have been injured as a result of your (or one of your employees') activities at work: for example, a brick dropped from scaffolding on passers-by.

Product liability insurance

This covers you for claims arising out of faults in something you or your employees have manufactured or serviced – if your folding chair collapses under a purchaser, say, or the washing-machine you have repaired gives a severe electrical shock.

Insurance for car and driver

Third-party insurance is, of course, compulsory on all the firm's vehicles; and you should insure at the same time for theft and accidents, etc. If your vehicles are going to be driven by various persons, make sure yours is an all-drivers policy.

If your work involves a great deal of driving, you would be wise to insure for loss of your driving licence, which could otherwise mean the loss of your livelihood. The insurance cannot restore your licence, but it can supply the means to hire a chauffeur.

Insurance if money is lost

A policy of this sort will cover you for loss of money (including cheques and postal orders) from your office, your till, from your house, or in transit – for instance, you could be robbed while taking it to the bank. Insurance can also be taken out to compensate an employee who is injured while being robbed of money.

Firms who hold clients' money, such as travel agents or insurance agents, need an insurance bond to protect them against loss if the business fails. Bonding is compulsory for some types of agency.

Personal insurance

You might consider private medical insurance. You could have some control over the timing of a non-urgent operation, so that it coincided with a slack business period, for example.

If you start a business alone, without a partner, an illness or accident which takes you out of circulation for any length of time could be damaging – or fatal – to your prospects. You can take out a policy, e.g. permanent health insurance, to cover these contingencies.

There is also a 'key person' insurance under which a limited company, a partnership or sole proprietor can obtain cover for loss of profit suffered as the consequence of the death of the proprietor, managing director, partner or senior employee. Any claim would be met either by a single lump sum or a number of annual instalments for some years following the death of the key person.

It is possible to get insurance to cover the cost of replacement personnel if a key person is called for jury service.

In a partnership, it is possible to get insurance for the eventuality of having to buy the partner's share in the business from his inheritors, in the event of the partner's death.

Other insurance

There is hardly a calamity for which you cannot insure your business or yourself. For instance, if you have a shop, you might enquire about a plate glass insurance policy, which would provide such facilities as having your broken window and/or door boarded up, speedy replacement of the glass, compensation for damage or injury by shattered glass, consequential loss of profits.

By becoming a member of the Federation of Small Businesses, 140 Lower Marsh, London SE1 7AE   TEL 071-928 9272, you are automatically entitled to insurance cover of up to £50,000 in these specific areas: expenses of VAT tribunal cases; awards made by industrial tribunals; Inland Revenue in-depth investigations and appeals against decisions under the 1985 Finance Act in respect of VAT. Further legal expenses insurance includes assistance with HSE cases, and motoring prosecutions, and a further benefit is a 24-hour telephone legal advice service.

Individual membership costs £60 a year (plus a joining fee of £20), and includes a bi-monthly magazine.

Brokers

You can never insure against anything, only for the cash compensation for any loss that you may suffer as a result of a happening. Insurance is a major industry, complex and rather specialised, so there may be a case for getting the advice of an insurance broker specialising in commercial insurance, particularly if you need some unusual type of insurance or if you are faced with what seem excessively high premium demands.

To find a good insurance broker, personal recommendation is likely to be best; or you might get in touch with BIIBA, the British Insurance and Investment Brokers' Association, BIIBA House, 14 Bevis Marks, London EC3A 7NT   TEL 071-623 9043, and ask for the names of some brokers willing to serve a small business, and make your choice from these. BIIBA also offers a free leaflet, *Small Firms Insurance*, which gives a brief checklist of the types of insurance that a small business may need.

CHAPTER 10

TIME TO GET A COMPUTER

THE JUSTIFICATION for getting a computer is to increase the efficiency of your business at least enough to offset the cost of installing and running the computer.

To assess your needs, start by making a list of all the areas in which a computer could be used in your business – for example, standard letters and circulars, costings, estimates and quotations, bookkeeping and preparation of accounts, invoices and statements, financial projections (including forecasting of cash flow and profit and loss), stock control, payrolls (including PAYE and National Insurance).

If you consider that a lot of your office work falls within these areas, give serious consideration to buying a computer. Even if you think you only need to go out and buy a typewriter, you may well find that you can buy a 'basic' (but nonetheless sophisticated) computer with word-processing software for rather less than the cost of a moderately sophisticated electronic typewriter.

A computer will be of assistance to almost any business, and is likely very quickly to justify itself either in financial terms or – perhaps equally importantly – in terms of saving your time.

Finding out about computers

Take your time in choosing a computer system. It is very important for you to acquire a system which does what you need it to do and which you find reasonably straightforward to operate. If you feel you are never going to come to grips with modern technology, then you should either steel yourself to go on an introductory course in the hopes that it will cure you of any phobias, or else leave the subject alone; you may however have a partner or a member of staff to whom the detailed investigation of the subject can be delegated. But, in any event, you are going to need a rudimentary understanding of the subject. The truth is that a computer must be treated as a slave rather than a master, moreover as a rather stupid slave which is only going to perform correctly if its master accustoms himself to giving it unambiguous instructions which he knows to be within its competence.

The individual investigating the possible purchase of a computer has the choice of calling in a computer consultant at the very start, or else of first learning something about the subject and then of taking more expert advice. The size of your business will determine the appropriate approach.

A larger business will be more likely to need, and to be able to justify the cost of employing, a computer consultant whose charges will be of the order of £60 to £100 per hour. Try to make sure you obtain the services of a reputable consultant. The consultant will need to know how your business works: while this is no doubt obvious to you, you may find it another matter to analyse it with sufficient clarity for an outsider to understand fully. If he or she considers that it is viable for your business to invest in a computer, advice will be given on appropriate systems.

A smaller business will almost certainly start by carrying out its own initial investigations. You (or, if appropriate, your partner or appointed investigator) can take the following steps at little or no cost:

If you have never had 'hands on' experience, your first session should be with word-processing, as this is akin to typing. A few minutes at a computer keyboard can be sufficient to allay ungrounded fears.

Get to understand the type of work that computers do, and also the computer market generally. Sources of information include:

- friends who work with computers
- other small businesses which are computerised
- computer courses: these range from brief introductory courses, some no longer than a day, to advanced subjects.

They are advertised in computer and business magazines. Your local university or college or adult education centre may also run classes

- computer books: there are many of these on the market; make sure that what you buy is at the appropriate level of expertise for yourself
- computer exhibitions, of which there are surprisingly many
- computer and business magazines: again, there are many of these and you should be able to find one or more at your level
- specialist shops (not the chain stores which sell computers – they tend to aim for the home computer market and are unlikely to offer more than a rudimentary expertise). Specialist shops usually sell a fairly limited range of hardware and software, and thus cannot be completely unbiased, but they tend to have a thorough knowledge of what they do sell
- the National Computing Centre, details obtainable from NCC, Oxford House, Oxford Road, Manchester M1 7ED (membership costs £350 a year)   TEL 061-228 6333
- the Federation of Information Systems Centres, an independent government-established body, with centres located throughout the UK. Details from Systems Information Technology Group, 3 Heaton Road, Newcastle upon Tyne NE6 1SA   TEL 091-276 6288.

What you need and the cost of buying it

The cost of a business computer starts at about £500; but the sky is the limit. In practice, you will probably find yourself spending about £1,200 on a reasonably up-to-date design with a hard disk giving substantial internal storage space for programs and information. However, the computer is only the first (albeit the most important) building block. In order to process and reproduce the information which you feed in, you must also buy:

- the program or programs which you intend to run on the computer – these are known generically as 'software'
- a printer (from £150)
- stationery – i.e., floppy disks, printer ribbons, continuous paper for the printer

- a maintenance contract – you need to know that if your computer breaks down it will be repaired as soon as possible, and, preferably, that a replacement can be made available until your machine is back in running order. Some programs come provided with a maintenance contract. This provides for the producer to resolve any 'bugs' or other problems encountered, and sometimes also to supply the customer with any updates to the program. Such a contract may cost (per annum) up to 15 per cent of the cost of the computer or software to which it relates. Call-out fees for the engineers are often charged in addition, in which case what you have bought with your maintenance contract is little more than the availability of specialised help. However, without it you might be in dire straits.

   Many new computer sellers offer warranties lasting from one to three years that you can buy at time of purchase. Find out whether an engineer will call on you if you have a problem.
- training for whoever is to use the computer – if the computer is to be used for management purposes (for example, for the accounts) you as proprietor of the business ought to have at least a nodding acquaintance with the program used. The cost of training – also of getting your computer up and running – may be an obligatory part of the 'package' cost if you are buying an entire system for a specialised purpose.

Few businesses will find themselves spending less than £1,500 on a computer system. The cost will, of course, depend on your requirements, but £2,500 may be considered a likely figure for many businesses. If this sounds a lot of money to spend, bear in mind that the price of computer equipment has been falling year by year, yet its quality and power are constantly improving. Moreover, a computer properly used may enable you to run your business with fewer staff than would otherwise be required.

Choosing the hardware

The term hardware means the machinery used in a computer system. It includes the computer itself and its peripherals, such as printers, modems (which enable computers to communicate with each other over telephone lines) and scanners (which copy documents).

Although the computer is only the first building block of a computer system, it will be by far the most important item bought, particularly since it will determine what programs are available to you. The most common of today's computers are 'clones' of the IBM PC originally introduced in 1981. All these 'IBM-compatibles' can run programs developed for the PC. Other computer systems, such as the Apple Macintosh or the Atari, have been developed independently with their own range of programs. IBM-compatibles are the jacks-of-all trades, with a massive range of software and compatible hardware available, while the others have a smaller range of software, much of it dedicated to specific areas, such as graphic design work or games playing.

You should buy a computer equipped with a hard disk with at least 40 megabytes (Mb) of memory. Your computer should also have at least 1Mb of RAM (random access memory – i.e. working memory) to ensure that it will be able to run the sophisticated programs now available, and at least 4Mb RAM if you want to run Windows (see 'Choosing the software').

Another vital consideration is the type of processor the computer has. This is the 'engine' of the system, determining its overall power and speed. Since 1981, successive generations of faster processors have been introduced. Currently the choice is between 386 and the faster, more expensive 486 processors; the earlier 286 generation is too slow to run much of today's software. 386 and 486 processors are further broken down into SX and the faster DX versions. Which processor you choose depends on what you need your computer to do: you will not need the speed and power of the 486 if all you want to do is write letters.

Various types of screen are available, and you should choose one to suit the programs you will be running. Use a VGA (video graphics array) or Super-VGA (S-VGA) screen with graphical user interfaces (see 'Choosing the software'). Less expensive types are suitable for text-only programs. Make sure the computer is fitted with a suitable 'video adaptor' card for the screen you want.

The cheapest type of printer is the dot matrix that forms print by using pins to strike a print ribbon. Ink jet printers are faster, quieter and give much better print quality. They form the print by aiming tiny bubbles of ink on to the page. At the top of the range, laser printers use a laser to magnetise a roller which attracts ink. The paper is then passed over the roller.

Once you have a computer, the door is open for you to use it in many ways you would not have originally intended, so it is a good idea to buy a system with enough memory and processing power to accommodate new programs in the future.

Choosing the software

The computer and its peripherals are the visible parts of the system. But without software – programs to tell them what to do – they can do nothing. There are two levels of software. On a low level is the operating software, which manages the computer's own resources. The most popular one is called MS-DOS, developed by Microsoft.

Graphical user interfaces (GUIs) were developed as an alternative to the text-based DOS by Apple (with its Macintosh computer), with the emphasis on making the computer easy to use. With GUIs, also known as mouse-and-pointer systems, the screen shows all of the software applications available as little pictures (known as icons), which you select by moving a hand-held unit called a mouse which in turn changes the position of a pointer on the screen. If you want to open up another program, you do not have to close down the one you are currently in, but can simply open up the second one in front of it. This 'multi-tasking' is more like non-computer work, where you don't have to put away one thing just to glance at another for a moment.

The most common GUI to be found on IBM-compatibles is Microsoft Windows, which puts a mouse-and-pointer system in front of MS-DOS, thereby bringing together the best of both personal computing worlds. The operating system software is usually included in the price of the computer.

On the higher level is applications software – the range of programs which carry out specific tasks, such as:

- word processing, for writing letters and creating documents
- accounting
- sophisticated information storage and processing systems known as 'databases'
- stock control
- financial planning
- communications, to send information to other computers.

There are also a number of 'integrated packages' which combine word processing, database, spreadsheet and communications functions, but these often need a great deal of computer power to run.

Your priority is to find the right software for your business needs. Almost every type of business has had software written for it at some time or other, and you will be best off using a tried and tested system if a suitable one is available. Make a point of asking how many other businesses use the same system, and try to arrange to see an existing system in operation before committing yourself.

Backing up data

Once a computer is turned off, all the information in the random access memory is lost. Therefore, if you want to keep your work, you will need to save it.

Floppy disks are small storage disks upon which you can save data. A built-in hard disk cuts this time down dramatically and is essential to run programs such as Windows.

Hard disks have high capacities and it is worth keeping all the programs you use frequently on hard disk to avoid the hassle of reloading them every time you want them.

Keep additional back-up copies of important files and your programs on floppy disk. Store back-ups away from the computer and update them regularly. Don't allow games or other non-business software to be used on the system as these may carry viruses – programs designed vindictively to destroy the data on your computer.

You can buy virus-killer programs (about £70) to combat viruses and check the health of your system. A tape streamer is a device which will back up the entire contents of your hard disk for secure storage. They are expensive (about £500), but invaluable if you simply cannot afford to lose your work.

Data protection

The Data Protection Act was passed in 1984 following widespread concern about people's private affairs being recorded on computers, with the attendant risks of inaccuracy and uncontrolled disclosure.

It is a very wide-ranging piece of legislation. It applies to information about living, identifiable individuals: not just sensitive information, but names, addresses and telephone numbers, even though these are to be found in directories. These data come under the Act if they are held in equipment which can process them automatically – for instance, a computer or word processor.

If you have a computer, you may need to register under the Act. A number of uses are exempt, for example, the home computer used not for business but for family affairs, household accounts and so forth. In business, there are several exempt uses (calculating pay, keeping accounts or basic text preparation) but the exemptions are hedged with strict conditions. If any of these conditions are breached, the exemption is lost. Separate legal entities will need to register individually.

You must find out whether you will need to register. An explanatory booklet with application forms is available direct from the Office of the Data Protection Registrar, Wycliffe House, Water Lane, Wilmslow, Cheshire SK9 5AF   TEL (0625) 535777.

You may need to register even if you do not have a computer of your own: your accountant, or a computer bureau, may hold and process data for you, but you control the contents and use of the data. If you have spare capacity on your computer which you make available to someone else, you will need to register as a computer bureau.

Failure to register is a criminal offence for which the Registrar can prosecute.

When registered, you must always operate within your register entry (such as purpose, type of data, source, to whom they are disclosed). This is important as it is also an offence under the Act to knowingly or recklessly hold or use data in a manner not described by your register entry. In addition, you must comply with the eight Data Protection Principles. If you change your business address, you must inform the Registrar.

The register is open to public inspection. Any individual about whom data is stored (that is, held on a computer), is entitled to a copy of the information concerning him or her. A charge of up to £10 (for each register entry searched) may be levied for giving access to the information, and there is a 40-day deadline for providing the information. Proper precautions must be taken to make sure that the individual requesting the information is who he or she claims to be. If an individual suffers damage (that is, financial loss, or physical injury – hurt feelings by themselves are not enough) as a result of his data being inaccurate, lost, destroyed or improperly disclosed, he or she is entitled to claim compensation.

Many trade associations and chambers of commerce have been studying the requirements, and may be able to advise you; so, of course, can your professional advisers. Ask your accountant to add data protection to the checklist for your business, to make sure that you operate as registered, and/or to notify the Registrar of any changes.

The current fee for registration is £75. Registration lasts for three years, after which time a renewal reminder will be sent automatically.

CHAPTER 11

PROTECTING IDEAS AND INNOVATION

ALL BUSINESSES own potentially valuable 'intellectual property' and ought therefore to know the simple procedures necessary to safeguard and use this property. Unfortunately, patents and other intellectual property rights are all too often ignored by small businesses because they are perceived as being complex and expensive. In fact, a business can avoid time-consuming problems and can save money simply by learning the basic rules of intellectual property.

Intellectual property primarily protects ideas and innovations against copying and imitation but, used properly, can do much more. For example, a company wishing to develop a new product should begin by having a patent search made. The patent specifications found will prevent the company from wasting time and effort 're-inventing the wheel' by repeating previous work. It is also possible for the search to reveal an ideal new product which is freely available for adoption.

Some intellectual property rights are true monopolies and provide protection against competition even when no copying has taken place. This means that a company initiating a new project quite independently could find itself being sued for infringement of the rights of others. If such conflict does arise, it will be necessary to withdraw from the market and to pay damages. The risk of coming into conflict with existing rights can largely be avoided by having 'freedom to use' searches made before any new product, service or logo is launched.

'Intellectual property' is the collective term used to refer to the laws designed to protect new ideas and innovations, namely:

- confidence
- copyright
- unregistered design right
- registered designs
- trade and service marks
- patents.

Confidence

All companies have information which they need to keep confidential. The recipe for Coca-Cola, for example, is a well-guarded secret. But more mundane company information, such as customer listings and next season's price list, needs to be kept from competitors.

To use confidentiality, it is necessary to identify the information which is to be kept secret. Access to the secret should be controlled, and those who are to know should be under a duty to maintain the confidence. Employees generally already have such a duty, but should be reminded of it. Outside contractors should be required to sign an appropriate undertaking to keep the information confidential.

Commonly, competitors seek access to databases such as customer lists and mailing lists. It is helpful to be alerted quickly to any misuse of such material, and therefore address lists, for example, may contain 'fake' entries to provide early warning of the use to which a list is being put.

Copyright and unregistered design right

You will have seen copyright notices, for example, at the end of television programmes, or when loading a computer program, but may still fail to appreciate that copyright impinges on all aspects of business. Copyright exists in the original 'literary, dramatic, musical or artistic work'. Literary works, for example, include computer programs, letters, booklets, advertisements, instruction manuals, price lists, business plans and databases. More physical objects such as buildings and sculptures, photographs and drawings also all have copyright.

Copyright is automatic. Any work which is original in the sense that someone has expended skill and effort in its production has copyright, and once the work has been completed the copyright is there. The company only needs to ensure that it owns copyright and that it can use it if necessary. This is simply a question of following the basic rules, which are:

- retain all original works
- ensure that all retained works identify the author and the date made
- ensure that the company owns the rights.

It is from the author of any piece of work that ownership of the copyright arises. If the author is an employee, and makes the work as part of his or her own duties, the company will own the copyright. Frequently though, advertising material, artwork, computer programs and other specialist works are contracted from outside. In such circumstances, agree at the outset who is to own any copyright which might arise, and record that agreement in writing.

Copyright is a right to prevent copying. If a competitor takes a short cut, for example, by issuing a leaflet which is the same or similar to one of your own, action can be taken to have the competitor's leaflet withdrawn and all copies destroyed. Furthermore, damages by way of compensation will be available. However, try to discourage copying by putting a copyright notice on original works made available to the public. Such a notice is the word 'copyright' or the symbol©, followed by the year of publication and the copyright owner's name.

Traditionally, manufactured products were also protected by copyright. However, since 1 August 1989, all such goods have been protected by a new right – the Unregistered Design Right (UDR). This provides limited protection for all manufactured goods, for example, for furniture, engineering products, tools, containers, clothing, toys and models, office equipment, packaging, jewellery, stationery, and consumer goods in general. UDR is similar to copyright in that it arises automatically and is a right to prevent copying or imitation. However, in most cases UDR will only last for ten years from first marketing, whereas copyright can exist for 50 years after the death of the author. As with copyright, a company has to ensure that it can enforce UDR if necessary. With UDR it is the original drawings or the first prototype of the new product which needs to be retained.

To avoid allegations of infringing copyright or UDR, make it a rule not to copy, and insist that products or services obtained from others are original. If a work is independently produced there can be no question of copyright infringement.

Registered designs

Although UDR provides some protection for industrial products, it is uncertain and is very limited in term. Therefore, reliance should not be put on this automatic protection for any projects of importance.

Where manufactured goods have a novel appearance, they can be protected by way of a registered design. This is a true monopoly, which can last for up to 25 years. To obtain a registered design it is necessary to go through an application process so that the Designs Registry, acting on behalf of the public, can satisfy itself that the application meets the necessary criteria.

To be granted a registered design it is a first requirement that the design is new, that is, that the product looks different from previous designs and has not already been sold or otherwise disclosed in the UK. This means that, in general, the application has to be filed before the product goes on to the market. However, in some cases it is still possible to obtain a valid design registration even after there has been some disclosure of the design, provided that less than 50 articles have been produced, and there have been no commercial dealings in the articles.

The second requirement is that the article should have been specifically designed to have an aesthetic appearance, or otherwise appeal to the eye. This is to exclude solely functional articles from registration. So, for example, office equipment and furniture which is sold on appearance is registrable, whereas functional items such as fuses and terminals are not.

Articles such as works of sculpture, wall plaques and medals, and printed matter such as calendars, greetings cards, maps, playing cards, etc. are specifically excluded from registration.

The application process to obtain a registered design is straightforward. It involves making a request for registration accompanied by drawings or photographs showing the article. It is considered by an Examiner of the Designs Registry and if there are no objections a Certificate of Registration is issued. Otherwise, the Examiner has to be persuaded by argument or amendment that any objections raised have been overcome.

When granted, a registered design enables the owner of the registration to stop anyone in the UK making, selling, using or importing articles with the same or similar design. The registration owner does not have to prove that the design has been copied, and it is immaterial that the infringement has been made independently.

Trade and service marks

A trade or service mark is a word or symbol telling not the nature of the goods, but their origin. Thus, if a book carries the trade mark 'Michelin' (TM), this does not mean that the book is made of rubber, nor is it about rubber products. The mark tells you that the French tyre company has originated or is in some way connected with the book.

Once a mark or brand has been chosen for goods and services, it is important, first of all, to ensure that the mark is free for use, that is, that using it will not infringe any existing rights. Thus, before a new mark is launched appropriate trade mark searches need to be carried out.

It is possible to acquire rights to a mark simply by using it, and where that use is so substantial that a considerable reputation has been built up, competitors can be stopped from using a similar mark by an action of 'passing off'. However, a strong brand is extremely valuable and ought to be protected even before goodwill and reputation have been accrued. This can be done by registering the mark.

In order to register a trade mark it is necessary to make an application to the Trade Marks Registry. A Trade Mark Examiner considers the application and, in particular, conducts searches to ensure that the proposed mark does not conflict with any existing registrations or applications in the pipeline. This means that an application for registration, and subsequently a registration, also prevents competitors registering similar marks and serves as a warning to others that you have rights to the mark.

Patents

Patents are the most powerful of all intellectual property rights. Like a registered design, a patent is a monopoly, but a patent protects much more than the visual appearance of an article. A patent can protect the basic concept of a project.

Patents protect 'inventions', that is, something that can be made or used in any kind of industry. This means that products, machines, methods of making products, testing products, and processes can all be protected by patents. However, a number of things are specifically excluded from patent protection, including discoveries, literary works, rules for playing games, methods of doing business and computer programs.

To obtain a patent the invention must be both new and non-obvious. An invention is new if, when a patent application is filed, it has not been made available in any way, to anyone, anywhere in the world. It is therefore vital to keep details of all projects confidential until it has been decided whether or not to apply for a patent.

An invention is 'obvious' if a person skilled in the field would think the invention trivial or an obvious development of what is already known. However, it is important not to confuse obviousness with simplicity. Patents are not necessarily about major breakthroughs, and many are granted every year for small improvements, for example, to fixings, packaging and other everyday products.

To be granted a patent it is necessary to go through an application procedure so that the Patent Office can establish that the necessary criteria for a patent have been met. This involves filing at the Patent Office a request for a patent together with a patent specification. This specification has to include a technical description which is in sufficient detail to enable someone to make or perform the invention. This means that published patent specifications are an extremely valuable source of technical information. The patent specification also has to include a definition of the protection required.

The patent application process is a step-by-step procedure, with the applicant having to initiate the various stages. During the procedure, an Examiner in the Patent Office makes a search through earlier patent documents to test the novelty of the proposal. Thereafter, the application is published to alert the public to its existence and to its contents. The final stage is essentially a negotiation process during which objections raised by the Patent Office have to be overcome by argument or amendment.

Patents are often ignored by business in the UK on the grounds that patents are complex and expensive, and that 'my competitor will easily be able to get round the patent by making minor changes'. In fact, patents are extremely powerful business tools and the cost of obtaining a patent in the UK to obtain an absolute monopoly for 20 years can be less than the insertion cost for one quarter page advertisement in a national newspaper.

Intellectual property outside the UK

Intellectual property is international and most countries provide rights which are very similar to those of the UK which are outlined above. Thus, copyright is recognised in most countries and action can generally be taken against plagiarists around the world using copyright which has been originated in the UK.

For registered designs and registered trade marks it is generally necessary to make a separate application in each country where protection is required. Fortunately, this does not need to be done at the same time that the UK application is filed. Thus, under the terms of the International Convention, foreign design or trade mark applications can be filed and can be given the date of the first British application if such foreign applications are made within six months of the first British application.

Generally, when seeking foreign rights it is necessary to apply in each country individually. However, two systems introduced in 1978 have made it easier to obtain foreign patents. First, there is the European system by which a single European patent can be obtained to cover up to 12 European countries, including the UK. Although the system is expensive it is a boon to those companies needing extensive protection in Europe. The International or PCT system enables a single application to be filed for up to 49 countries. This system is extremely useful as it enables any expenditure on foreign applications to be delayed for 18 months whilst the project is commercialised.

There are plans to provide both a Community patent and a Community trade mark. However, it is more than likely that most small businesses will have no need for Community-wide protection, especially as it will be expensive, and the national rights will continue to meet their needs.

Getting help

The UK Patent Office publishes free information as to how to obtain patents, designs and trade marks, and this is available on request from its London office, Department of Trade and Industry, 25 Southampton Buildings, London WC2A 1AY TEL 071-438 4700. However, it is generally advisable to seek professional help and guidance.

The professionals who are qualified to advise in all intellectual property rights are patent agents or patent attorneys. Their professional body is the Chartered Institute of Patent Agents, Staple Inn Buildings, High Holborn, London WC1V 7PZ TEL 071-405 9450. The Chartered Institute can provide free introductory booklets on patents, trade and service marks, and industrial designs.

You can find a patent agent from *Yellow Pages* or from a regional directory available free from the Chartered Institute. But do make sure that you are dealing with a Chartered Patent Agent (CPA). Anyone, including the unqualified, is able to offer services in these areas.

A patent agent can apply for any of the intellectual property rights for you, can make searches to see if ideas are new, and to check your freedom to use new ideas and innovations, and can advise and act if things go wrong. Patent agents can also advise on agreements, licensing and other commercial dealings with such rights. Many firms of patent agents are also prepared to offer free preliminary advice, for example, under the Chartered Institute's scheme 'Patent Agents for Innovation'.

If you wish to make patent searches yourself, the British Library Science Reference and Information Service, 25 Southampton Buildings, London WC2A 1AW   TEL 071-323 7919, has a comprehensive collection of British and foreign patents. Patent collections are also held in patent libraries in Birmingham, Glasgow, Leeds, Liverpool, Manchester, Newcastle upon Tyne and Sheffield.

A good practical description of intellectual property and how it can be used for commercial advantage will be found in *Intellectual Property – A Manager's Guide,* Ed. Vivien Irish, 1991 McGraw-Hill.

CHAPTER 12

BEING A RETAILER

EVERY high street is the same – every high street is different: paradoxically, both statements are true. From town to town, the first impression is of sameness, with the familiar chain stores and multiples, Boots, W H Smith, Sainsbury's and many others in various combinations in every shopping centre of any size. But if you look more closely, you will notice among the famous fascias many belonging to the smaller businesses, with just the one shop, or perhaps one or two branches. And in villages and suburban shopping parades the individual businesses will be in the majority; some old-established, others recently started, all determined to keep their end up.

These are not easy times for retail businesses: the shopkeepers are fighting the huge organisations for a share of the customers' spending power, and are using considerable ingenuity in doing so. The multiples, with their enormous resources, vast floor space and the ability to command the whole output of a factory, have an undoubted advantage in cutting prices and offering a large variety of lines. The smaller shops that do not evolve and adapt to meet this challenge are fighting tanks with bows and arrows.

Some practise guerrilla warfare, turning their small size to advantage in offering kinds of service that are not worth the big organisations' while: opening very early or staying open very late; delivering to customers' houses; and various others. The small shop's strongest weapon is the element of service which is the one thing the giants cannot match. Many people prefer to spend their money where vegetables and groceries will be delivered, a dress altered to fit exactly, d-i-y tools sold with some expert advice.

The small shop can sell goods in small quantities: one slice of ham, half a yard of elastic, six screws; in the big stores, such items are prepacked, giving the customer little control over quantity. Such a service is especially valuable to people whose needs are modest.

Having what it takes

Most people have idyllic childhood memories of playing shop: reality is quite a bit different.

It helps to be an early riser (especially in the food trade), such as a greengrocer who has to go to the wholesalers in the early hours, and be back in time to open the shop. Or there may be early morning deliveries to attend to, as in the case of a newsagent. You may not get to bed very early either, because accounts, stock control, VAT, ordering, credit card matters may all have to be dealt with in the evening.

The advice that you should acquire some working experience before setting up on your own applies doubly to shopkeeping, not only in order to learn some of the mechanics of the trade but to find out if you are temperamentally suited to it.

If your customers become irate, you will hear about it pretty soon. But no matter how you feel, you will have to appear unfailingly cheerful, patient, polite, and helpful even when customers offer a good deal of provocation. An offended customer is unlikely to return.

Opening hours

The trading hours of shops are still regulated by the Shops Act 1950, the gist of which is that shops may open at whatever time they like, but must close by 8pm on weekdays and 9pm on one weekday night (late shopping night). Shops may open on Sundays to sell a limited range of goods: newspapers, magazines, cigarettes, tobacco, sweets, milk, fresh vegetables, cooked food and various other items, usually of a perishable nature, or related to entertainment (guide books, postcards) or emergencies (medi-cines, surgical appliances).

Shops must close by 1pm one day a week (not necessarily all on the same one) unless the majority of the shopkeepers in the district petition for this regulation to be relaxed. Some shops are exempt from the early closing rule: the criteria are roughly the same as for Sunday opening.

There are relaxations for shops in holiday areas, which may stay open on some Sundays to sell holiday goods (e.g., camera film, fishing rods). Some shops owned by Jews which close on Saturdays may open on Sundays.

You will probably have noticed the law about shop hours being broken. Many local authorities take a relaxed attitude to this, especially when the shop is staffed by members of the owner's family. It is as well to find out your own local authority's stand, if you plan to stay open outside the prescribed hours.

Premises for a retail business

There is one common factor shared by almost all retail busi-nesses: the need for a street frontage. Generally this means that the shopkeeper must find ready-built premises in a shopping centre (though if it is a new development, he or she may be the first occupier).

A trader needs to choose the right shop in the right location in the right district, and adapt it to his or her own needs.

Choosing the district
It is doubtful whether anybody chooses an area in which to trade completely at random. You, too, will probably have reasons of your own for wishing to open a shop in one part of town rather than another.

By all means use your inclination as a starting point, but keep an open mind: if your investigations show that the preferred district is a no-hoper, look elsewhere.

Find out, preferably by personal investigation over a period of time, whether the area is prosperous or declining. Try to find out what the unemployment rate is: closed-down factories are an ominous sign. Note 'For Sale' boards on private houses – if there are many, and they remain for a long time, there may be more people moving away from the area – or trying to – than are coming in. If there are many high-street shops for sale or rent, you will not have any trouble finding one, but you may not do much trade there.

Look at what other shopping centres there are near by. It may be that the more prosperous residents, the ones with cars, are accustomed to take their business farther away, perhaps to some big, new shopping complex, so that you would have to make do with the shoppers who cannot manage or afford the journey.

Do people come to work in the district? Look for offices, schools, colleges, industrial estates: people who have to shop in their lunch hour seldom go far afield. On the other hand, if you mostly sell to people who commute in, you may be twiddling your thumbs on Saturdays, which elsewhere are the best shopping days.

Where there are any other reasons why people should come into the district – a swimming-pool, a central library, council offices, a museum or art gallery – all these can bring in potential customers from other districts. If there is a railway station or bus terminus near by, the users may have to pass by.

Choosing the location

For a shop, nothing is more important than location. For most, the more prominent the location, the better, because although much of the custom may come from regulars, a good deal comes from passers-by, who are lured in on impulse.

A small shop in a small suburban shopping parade probably enjoys little passing trade and may have a captive clientele of local residents, particularly the mothers of young families, and the elderly. By staying open later than the high-street shops, it may attract people who work and those who have simply run out of something. If this is the sort of shop you want, finding premises will be largely a question of locating a vacant property. But be careful about competition: there may not be enough trade for two butchers or two hardware merchants.

In a high-street shopping centre, the presence of a competing business may not necessarily be a disadvantage; it can even be a good thing, up to a point.

Where there are several shops of the same kind in a shopping district, it encourages people to travel there; customers like the prospect of choice, an alternative source near by: that source could be your shop. For some kinds of shop, competition is a positive factor: bookshops and shoe shops, for instance. Book-buyers like to drift from shop to shop, browsing: a shoe customer will prefer to know that if the shoes he or she wants are not available in one shop, there is another shoe shop near by. Estate agents, too, gain a collective benefit from being closely associated with each other – people tend to visit a number of agencies, so there is no harm in making it easy for them.

A specialist shop, such as a builder's merchant, or a musical instrument shop, whose custom hardly depends on passing trade, may do well enough in a side street: it will attract specialist customers by becoming known in the trade.

Every shopping street has its 'dead end', where the trade is slower and the shops are less prosperous and change hands more often. It is important to identify and shun this unlucky location (probably marked by a rash of For Sale and To Let boards).

Even in the 'live' part of the street, some locations can be better than others. If you are taking over a going concern, you have, obviously, less choice. But if you are buying or, more probably, renting, vacant property to convert to your own use, give preference to one sited where people have to pause: next to a pedestrian crossing, a bus stop, near a parking place.

Buying a going concern

If you decide to take over a shop which is at present trading, the first thing you will want to find out is the owner's reasons for selling. They may be genuinely personal – such as ill health, or retirement. Or they may be strategic: perhaps the owner has heard rumours of a huge new supermarket to be built nearby, or of a large local factory closing down, and is getting out while the going is good. Find out by questions to the planning authorities, and enquiries in the neighbourhood, what new developments are planned in the area. A new main road bisecting a shopping district can halve its trade. Designating roads as one-way can be almost equally bad for trade, as it discourages some traffic from entering the area. A new hypermarket or shopping precinct could be fatal.

Or perhaps the present owner simply has not been able to make a success of the business, in which case the question is – can you? You should not only scrutinise the shop's accounts, but, if possible, also observe the proprietor at work. The reason for his poor financial performance may be idleness, incompetence, understocking or overstocking, understaffing or overstaffing, poor choice of goods or of opening hours. Perhaps it is the location that is at fault, and no shop in that line of business could succeed there.

There are other considerations: if the fixtures and fittings are not to your liking, how much will it cost to refit the shop? There may be no choice whether to buy or rent the premises. When renting, which is more common, you must know how long the lease has to run, whether it is renewable and on what terms. In a repairing lease, the consequent dilapidation liability must be allowed for in financial planning.

There is also the problem of what the goodwill is worth. A shop which is doing poorly cannot claim much of that, but even if it is doing well you cannot be sure that the customers are regulars who will transfer their custom to you.

You will, of course, have the property valued by a professional valuer and its leases and accounts thoroughly inspected, before coming to a decision.

These considerations are discussed in more detail earlier in this book.

Starting a new business

You may be looking for an empty property in order to start a completely new shop. Where such a property is brand-new, in a newly built development, it may be difficult to assess your potential custom. But you should at least inspect the district; ideally, the development should include new housing or be near a residential area or a commuter area.

If you are thinking of taking over empty premises previously used as a shop, find out why the previous owner closed down:

perhaps this is one of those 'dead' sites where no business ever succeeds.

You will have to clear any change of use with the local authority's planning department. But if you intend to carry on a business of a similar character to the previous one, there is likely to be no problem. Most retail businesses are considered as interchangeable, and you can freely convert from one kind to another without permission. However, if you carry out any structural alterations to the building, your plans must be approved in the usual way.

You should consult your fire prevention officer and some kinds of businesses, such as garages, which have special fire hazards, have their own regulations.

Accepting credit cards

If your goods carry a profit margin reasonably in excess of the credit card companies' commission (at present around 4 to 5 per cent for smaller businesses), you may decide to try to attract more customers by becoming a merchant of one or all of the principal credit card organisations: American Express, Diners, Mastercard (e.g., Access) or Visa (e.g., Barclaycard, Trustcard).

When you have signed an agreement with a credit card company, you will be supplied with vouchers, an imprinter and instructions on the acceptance of cards.

Certain checks are necessary every time a card is presented: making sure the card is valid (the expiry date has not passed); that the card has not been notified to you as lost or stolen; that the amount is within the 'floor limit' advised to you by the credit card company (if it is in excess, you will need to obtain authorisation); and that the signature of the customer on the sales voucher agrees with the signature on the card. Details of the card are then recorded on the voucher by use of the imprinter.

You may be given an envelope in which to send your vouchers to the card company; or you may, in the case of Visa and Mastercard, hand them over to a cashier at a bank as you would cash or cheques, in which case your account will be immediately credited with the full amount of the value of the transactions. You will receive a monthly statement from the credit card company, summarising all the transactions submitted, and indicating the service charge due, which will be deducted from your account by direct debit.

Credit card trading is not appropriate to some forms of retail trade, such as small food shops or others where the margin of profit is low, because of the credit card company's service charge or commission.

Accepting luncheon vouchers

If you sell pre-prepared food in any form, from full restaurant meals to snacks and sandwiches, and you want to accept Luncheon Vouchers, you have to make sure that they are used for food only, though the term 'food' includes any component of a bona fide meal, such as a canned drink. The address of Luncheon Vouchers Limited is 50 Vauxhall Bridge Road, London SW1V 2RS TEL 071-834 6666. The organisation will send you full details and display signs for your windows.

You have to count the vouchers and take them or send them to the company for reimbursement. There is a service charge on the redemption of the vouchers; this varies from 1.2 per cent to 1.7 per cent, depending on the volume. In exchange, Luncheon Vouchers guarantees payment in nine working days, and also pays for the postage and insurance of the parcel in transit.

Buying stock

This is the heart of the matter for any shopkeeper who invests a large proportion of capital in stock, and, therefore, must buy it wisely.

How much to stock

Some products deteriorate rapidly (flowers, bread, greengroceries); others do not spoil with keeping, but go out of fashion (clothes, shoes). Even when they neither spoil nor date (most hardware), if nobody buys them, they bring in no profit with which to buy new stock, and take up the space needed for this stock. So, in every case, a rapid turnover of stock is desirable. Stock unsold is cash tied up or lost.

Do not be tempted to over-stock, perhaps by an attractive quantity discount, nor to diversify too much.

The ideal is to buy only what your customers want, and to buy no more of it than you are able to sell.

You could buy through a symbol group, if you belong to one; or from a wholesaler; or from a cash-and-carry warehouse (a kind of retailers' supermarket); or directly from a manufacturer. They are not mutually exclusive. You might think that your orders are unlikely to be large enough to qualify for the quantity discounts which the manufacturer makes available to buying organisations and wholesalers, but do not dismiss the idea of buying direct from manufacturers.

Symbol groups

Some shopkeepers, particularly in the grocery trade, take on the big battalions with their own weapons by joining a voluntary symbol group which is a retailers' buying organisation (such as VG, Spar, Mace, Wavy Line) in order to secure the large discounts that manufacturers offer to bulk-buyers.

The retailer agrees to take a certain amount of goods each week from the designated wholesaler for his or her area and receives better terms than he would get on his own, and possibly other advantages such as a fascia with the group's symbol and the shop's name, help with the layout and fixtures. In some cases, start-up help is given: the wholesaler may give the newcomer help in finding a shop and finance for it.

Details of the relevant head offices and wholesalers are listed in the Grocer Marketing Directory available from the publishers, William Reed Ltd, Broadfield Park, Crawley, West Sussex   TEL (0293) 613400 (or try your reference library). The trade press, mainly grocery, but also, for example, hardware, carries such information. The applicant shopkeeper must offer some evidence of financial security, such as a bank reference. If he or she is already in business, the wholesaler will inspect the premises to see that they are in line with the organisation's requirements.

If there are other shops belonging to the particular symbol group in the neighbourhood, the wholesaler may refuse to take on another.

Members of the group must undertake to purchase more than a specific amount regularly, and to stock a certain number of the organisation's own-brand products, but are free to buy goods from agencies other than the designated wholesaler.

Buying direct or from wholesalers?

When you first open your shop, if you are in a price-competitive field, it is important to try to open with a bang, not a whimper. Your opening offers should be good, and as the initial stocking of the shop is likely to be your largest single stockbuying for a long time, you may qualify for a quantity discount on this order. This is also the time to establish contact with the representatives of the major firms (probably four to eight) whose products are likely to account for a large part of your turnover. The manufacturers' representatives will have a good idea of what are competitive retail prices for the particular products, and may help you to reach them by means of promotional allowances or by providing redeemable 'money off' coupons for customers.

Obviously, you must check that you are not overlooking other sources of supplies that are cheaper, by joining a symbol group and finding a good cash-and-carry source.

Plan your opening carefully: there is no second chance to make a good first impression. Choose about twenty top selling lines and be prepared for very low profit margins on these. They can be from a mixture of sources; choose the best items from each.

When stocking your shop initially, you may be able to negotiate extended credit from your supplier, perhaps no payment for two months, then one-sixth of your opening order to be paid for over the following six months.

An advantage of dealing direct with the manufacturer is that if there are damages, the reps have facilities for exchange or credit which a symbol group or cash-and-carry store may not afford to you. A keen rep can use these facilities to give the retailer a little extra discount on his purchases. You should be aware that damages eat into profit margins just as outdated stock does.

It is possible that manufacturers are less likely to run out of stock than a buying group – and lost sales lead to lost customers. But an advantage of indirect buying, if you stock many items, is cutting down on the time it takes to accept and check deliveries: much of your stock will arrive on one van, or, in the case of a cash-and-carry, be collected by you from one address. There will also be a considerable saving in paperwork.

What to stock?

There is, of course, no single answer to the question of which products and lines you ought to stock. It is partly common sense, partly flair, and partly experience – so here, too, it helps to have worked in the trade.

Customers hardly ever give prior notice of their wants, but expect to find what they want when they want it. And if it is not there in your shop, they go somewhere else, rather than wait for it to be ordered. So the shopkeeper must keep on his toes, trying not to run out of anything, especially the most popular lines.

This demands keeping proper records and a constant check on what goes out, plus efficient and far-sighted reordering, which takes account of the fact that manufacturers do not always meet delivery dates, and that wholesalers have been known to run out of some products. A computer with the appropriate software can help in stock control (and at the same time indicate the profitability of various types of stock).

You must store your stock in such a way that it deteriorates as little as possible and does not acquire that grubby, shopworn look which is so off-putting to customers.

You must rotate it, making sure that articles bought at the earliest period are put on sale first. Some food products are marked with 'sell by' dates, or shelf-life limits, and become unsaleable once these dates are passed.

Goods which have failed to sell or have passed the peak of saleability should be marked down in price, or thrown away, if perishable. Apart from taking up space fruitlessly, they create a bad impression. You might hold a seasonal sale or sell off unwanted stock week by week, or even day by day, depending on the type of goods.

Display

When you think of shops, you think of windows, their distinguishing feature. No other kind of business depends so much on visual display to attract customers.

What is essential is that the display should appear fresh, uncluttered and up to date: not dusty, crowded and superannuated. The window should be well-lit, as eye catching as possible, and changed fairly often. If there is any item that you want to promote specially, it should have pride of place.

Prices should be clearly marked, whenever possible. Leaving off price tickets does not encourage people to come inside to ask the price: it is more likely to make them suspicious and put them off.

If you decide to make your shop self-service, the goods must be easily accessible and each article marked with its price. And you must make sure that the check-out will not create a bottleneck.

When you acquire a shop, the previous owner's fixtures and fittings may suit your purpose exactly, but it is more probable that you will want to make some changes, if only by redecorating. If you are changing the nature of the shop's trade, you will want to start from scratch.

Plan this carefully beforehand, making a list of your requirements and a provisional sketch of the layout; then get estimates from several firms of specialist shopfitters, choosing the one that offers the best value for money. Visit any relevant trade exhibitions, such as Shopex which is held every June at Olympia, London, that concentrates on shopfitting, self-service and display equipment. Use your buying group facilities and choose the best that you can afford. Fittings have to last a long time and penny-pinching at the initial stage might prove expensive later.

Shopbreaking

You cannot make your shop burglar-proof, but you can make it harder to burgle. Before you start trading, consult the crime prevention officer at your local police station, and perhaps get a good security firm to inspect the premises and install all necessary devices: locks and/or bolts on all doors and windows (not forgetting the basement and the attic); burglar alarms, not so sensitive that they go off all the time; and anything else that seems sensible. But make sure that what you do does not conflict with the fire prevention regulations.

Other precautions include great attention to locking up; every key accounted for at all times; a light left on all night. Do not leave money in the till overnight; leave the till open at night – a thief would open it anyway, causing unnecessary damage – most insurance companies insist on this. Do not have large sums of money in the shop at any time. Send someone to the bank with it. After banking hours, use the night safe.

You should have adequate insurance from the beginning of trading. If you do happen to be burgled, good stock control will pay off, as you will find it easier to list what has been stolen, which will help in getting your claim settled more promptly.

Pilferage by staff

This can be anything from a hand in the till to stealing from stock. By and large, it is the bigger firms' problem: supermarkets have the highest rate of shrinkage. The small shop run by the owner and his family needs less internal protection. But there should be rules about employees' own purchases from the shop.

Although it is difficult to know who is trustworthy, you should be as discriminating as possible about whom you employ. Demand, and take up, references. It is a nerve-racking business and not likely to improve relations with staff, having to practise eternal vigilance, constantly checking the deliveries, the stock, the till. Experience will help to teach you what precautions are necessary.

Shoplifting

This is more of a problem if the shop has a self-service layout, or if the goods are displayed on stands or racks (as in many clothes shops). You will hardly be able to afford to employ a shop detective, but it might be worthwhile to consider renting a closed-circuit TV system; you will get back some of the cost in tax relief. Often the presence itself of such a system is a deterrent. Place the monitor screen so that it can also be seen by customers.

Strategically placed mirrors, perhaps convex ones, can help at a modest cost. The shop itself should be well lit, with no murky corners, and shelves or racks of goods should have full light on them.

Expensive pocketable items can be chained to the stands: perhaps electrically connected so that a buzzer sounds if the chain is removed.

Advice on these and other anti-theft devices can be sought from a security firm specialising in shop protection.

Vigilance is essential, but however suspiciously a customer may be behaving, do not challenge him or her until they have removed an article from the premises. Only if theft has taken place, and you have good grounds for suspecting who did it, can you make a citizen's arrest of a shoplifter. If you 'arrest' someone and then he or she is acquitted, so that no theft has been proved to have taken place, the arrest would be unlawful and you could be made to pay heavy damages.

'Dud' cheques

When you accept a cheque, there is always a possibility that it may bounce, unless you insist on the production of a cheque card, and write its number down on the back of the cheque. This guarantees payment if you took the cheque in good faith, and you can insist on the bank paying up, to a set limit (either £50 or £100) even if the chequebook and card should turn out to have been stolen, or if the customer's account is empty. Some shops are willing to take two or three cheques for single purchases costing over the limit, but this invalidates the bank's guarantee of the cheque card, and possibly none of the part-payment cheques would be honoured.

Do not accept any other identification, such as a driving licence, since it does not guarantee the owner's solvency. Do not accept cheques for more than the limit stated on the card without checking with the customer's bank, or holding up delivery of the goods until the cheque has been cleared.

Credit card fraud

The holders of credit cards, such as Barclaycard, Access, American Express, Diners Club, are supposed to notify the issuing organisation as soon as they discover a card to have been lost or stolen. If you accepted a stolen card in good faith, however, the issuing organisation will pay you the money. The credit card company may send you details of stolen cards from time to time, with instructions not to accept those cards. The number of cards which you are asked to check at any one time is kept to a minimum – but it may still be difficult for a shop to check every single card that is offered.

Card companies pay rewards for lost or stolen cards which are picked up by shops, but may refuse to accept transactions resulting from the use of cards which have been listed as stolen.

Learning the law

The shopkeeper must comply with a number of laws, both civil (such as the Sale of Goods Act 1979, the Unfair Contract Terms Act 1977 and the Supply of Goods and Services Act 1982) and criminal (such as the Trade Descriptions Act 1968 and the Fair Trading Act 1973). The Consumer Protection Act 1987 deals with certain civil and criminal matters.

Other relevant criminal legislation includes the Food Safety Act 1990 and the Weights and Measures Act 1985: these form a series of special rules and regulations which apply to food.

All these pieces of legislation aim at enforcing the principles of fair trading. Advice can be sought from each local Trading Standards Department.

Sale of Goods Act 1979

The sale of goods legislation has guided the relationship between the seller and the buyer for nearly a century. The Sale of Goods Act 1893 was the first piece of legislation actually to set down in writing the legal position existing between the seller and the buyer in a contract for the sale of goods, and now, the Sale of Goods Act 1979 provides the foundation of the present law relating to the sale of goods. The 1979 Act gives protection to each buyer by implying certain rights or terms (known as conditions) into every contract for the sale of goods. The most important of these are that:

- the goods correspond with the description applied to them – whether orally, or on the container, packaging, wrapping, labelling or other advertising;
- the goods are of merchantable quality – that is, that they work properly, are in a satisfactory state, and are suitable for the ordinary, everyday purpose for which goods of that kind are usually bought;
- the goods are fit for the particular purpose – that is, not only must they work properly and be well-made, but fit for the particular purpose that the buyer wants them for, whether that is an ordinary, everyday purpose or an extraordinary or unusual one. For example, a carpet may be of merchantable quality but quite unsuitable for use in a specific location; but when the shopkeeper sells it to meet a specific requirement, it must be reasonably fit for the purpose specified. If the shopkeeper does not know whether or not the commodity will meet the customer's specific needs, he or she should make it clear that they do not know and therefore cannot advise the buyer.

Second-hand, reduced and shop-soiled goods are all protected by the requirement of the Sale of Goods Act. Such goods may be imperfect, but the buyer is entitled to fair value for the money he or she has paid for them.

The shopkeeper, too, is afforded some measure of protection, and the buyer has no right to claim that goods are unmerchantable where:

- the shopkeeper specifically drew the buyer's attention to the faults or defects being complained about before the sale was made, *or*
- the buyer examined the goods before the sale was made and should have seen the faults or defects being complained about for himself or herself.

Breach of any of these conditions amounts to a breach of contract, and it is for the shopkeeper to put the matter right between the customer and himself or herself. The customer is entitled to reject the goods, to reclaim the purchase price in full and to claim compensation for any loss or damage that has happened as a direct result of the contract being broken, such as the cost of re-papering and painting where a faulty cooker has exploded causing damage to the kitchen walls and ceiling. Afterwards, the shopkeeper can make a similar claim against the supplier or the manufacturer, being now the aggrieved party.

The Limitation Act 1980 allows the buyer to bring a court action for breach of contract against the shopkeeper at any time up to six years from the date when the cause of action first arises (usually, the date of purchase). The same time limit covers actions between the shopkeeper and the supplier for breach of contract. Where there is nothing wrong with a product as regards description, quality or fitness, and the buyer simply changes his or her mind about it, there is no legal obligation on the part of the shopkeeper to give a refund, or even an exchange. If the shopkeeper does so, it is purely a gesture of goodwill.

Unfair Contract Terms Act 1977

The Unfair Contract Terms Act is concerned, in part, with restricting or preventing the shopkeeper from avoiding his or her liability towards a customer by using exclusion clauses in contracts. Attempts to exclude liability for goods which do not fit their description, are not fit for the purpose for which they were bought, and are not of merchantable quality, are void under the Act. In contracts with traders, the effectiveness of such exclusion clauses depends on whether a court regards them as reasonable. In all contracts, any clause excluding liability for death or personal injury caused by negligence is void. Clauses excluding other liability for negligence can be assessed as reasonable or not.

Other clauses subject to a reasonableness test are those which try to get out of accepting liability for the loss of articles left for servicing, or for the late delivery of goods which were promised by a certain time.

The Act, however, allows an exclusion clause in dealings between the shopkeeper and the manufacturer, but only where that clause is a reasonable one. The Act itself sets out guidelines as to the test of reasonableness to be applied, and if a manufacturer wishes to rely on any particular exclusion clause, the burden of proof will be placed on him or her to show that the clause is fair and reasonable in the circumstances.

Supply of Goods and Services Act 1982

The Supply of Goods and Services Act brings into statute law the various sorts of protection which the consumer has previously enjoyed under common law. Goods supplied as part of a service, on hire, or in part exchange, must fulfil the same conditions (such as being of merchantable quality, fit for the purpose, conforming to description) as the Sale of Goods Act lays down for goods that are being sold.

The Act also sets out clearly that the customer should be able to expect any service he pays for to be carried out with reasonable care and skill, within a reasonable time and at a reasonable price (unless a fixed time or a fixed price has already been agreed between the parties).

Where the service takes the form of a particular skill – such as, for example, a hairdresser providing a 'cut and blow-dry' – the reasonable standard of care and skill required would be that expected of a reasonably competent member of the hairdressing profession. The work done in providing the service must have been authorised by the customer, and the retailer cannot expect payment for work done over and above what had been agreed between the customer and himself or herself.

In Scotland the same consumer rights exist but are covered by common law.

Further reading

Booklets giving an outline of the basic consumer rights can be obtained from the Office of Fair Trading, Room 306, Field House, 15–25 Bream's Buildings, London EC4A 1PR   TEL 071-242 2858.

Although nominally addressed to shoppers, the booklets contain much useful information for traders, about their various obligations to customers.

Croner's Reference Book for Self-employed and Smaller Business, Croner House, London Road, Kingston upon Thames, Surrey KT2 6SR TEL 081-547 3333, includes explanatory notes on selected Acts of Parliament. It has a loose-leaf format, and the price, £116.40, includes a monthly updating service in the form of replacement pages, and postage and packing; in subsequent years, this costs £89.85 including postage and packing.

Law for Retailers, by Jennifer Brave, published by Sweet & Maxwell, sets out the key areas of law as they apply to retailers, and contains details of legislation of direct relevance to retailers, including sale of goods, trade descriptions, bargain offers, credit, consumer safety, theft and related offences, and negligence.

Receipts

The practice of giving the customer a written receipt as proof of purchase is a fundamental one to the retail business, but at common law there is no legal obligation on the part of the retailer to give a receipt, nor for the customer to produce one. The absence of a written receipt does not mean that the goods have not been paid for – the receipt could have been lost, or the shopkeeper may have omitted to give one in the first place. The law allows the shopper to prove his purchase not only by written proof (such as a till receipt or the customer portion of a credit card voucher) but also verbally (by 'parole evidence' – simply stating that he or she bought the items from that retailer). If payment is made by cheque, the law regards a cheque as a receipt, once it has been paid by the bank.

That is why the law forbids the shopkeeper to put up notices and display signs, or their equivalent, saying such things as: 'Refunds cannot be given in the absence of a written receipt', which imply to the customer that complaints will be dealt with only on written proof of purchase. Statements like this are illegal, and the shopkeeper cannot rely on them.

Fair Trading Act 1973

The criminal law imposes further limits or restrictions on the shopkeeper relating to statements he or she may wish to make to customers, by virtue of the Consumer Transactions (Restrictions on Statements) Orders 1976 and 1978. These also apply to the manufacturer of goods, and have their origin in the Fair Trading Act 1973.

The Orders make it a criminal offence for a shopkeeper or a manufacturer to 'cut out' the statutory rights – as to merchantable quality, fitness for the particular purpose, and conforming to description – afforded to the customer by the Sale of Goods Act 1979, whether by means of a display notice, a written contract, a wrapper, label, packaging, advertisement, or the goods themselves.

For this reason, each of the following statements is illegal and you can be prosecuted in respect of each of them: 'no money refunded', 'for hygiene purposes, goods cannot be returned or money refunded', 'sale goods, no money refunded', and 'credit notes only for faulty goods'.

Breach of the Orders is a criminal offence, which is punishable by fine, imprisonment or both. Enforcement in each locality is carried out by the Trading Standards or Consumer Protection Department.

Trade Descriptions Act 1968

The law of trade descriptions is of tremendous importance. Breach of it is a criminal offence, punishable by fine, imprisonment or both. Enforcement is the duty of the local Trading Standards or Consumer Protection Department, whose duly authorised officers have power to make test purchases, to enter premises and inspect and seize goods and documents for the purpose of determining whether or not the law is being complied with. Respect should be shown for their office, which, incidentally, dates as far back as Magna Carta. Any person who wilfully obstructs a Trading Standards Officer, or who wilfully fails to comply with a valid request by such an Officer, or who without reasonable cause fails to give any other assistance asked for, commits the offence of obstruction.

Trading Standards Officers will also be pleased to provide guidance and advice, should you wish to consult them.

The 1968 Act creates a basic set of criminal offences by generally prohibiting false trade descriptions. It makes it an offence for a shopkeeper to describe goods falsely and to sell, or offer for sale, goods so misdescribed. It applies to all aspects of retailing and includes advertisements, display cards, illustrations, labelling, packaging, brochures, ticketing and statements made verbally.

It covers descriptions as to quality, quantity, size, method or process of manufacture, composition, performance, fitness for purpose, testing, approval by any person, previous history of the goods, place or date of manufacture or processing, and by whom made.

Section 14 of this Act makes it a criminal offence for the trader to make a statement which he knows is false relating to the provision of services, accommodation and facilities. For instance, if a trader provided an invoice stating he had carried out certain repairs to goods and these have not been carried out, an offence may have been committed under this section.

If things go wrong, and proceedings have been taken against the shopkeeper for supplying or offering to supply goods to which a false trade description is applied, he has a defence if he can prove that he did not know, and could not with reasonable diligence have found out, that the goods did not match the description, or that the description had been applied to the goods in question.

The shopkeeper also has a defence in cases where an offence has been committed through mistake or an accident, or through reliance on information supplied to him, or through the act or default of another person, or some other cause beyond his (the shopkeeper's) control. He must show that he 'took all reasonable precautions' *and* 'exercised all due diligence' to avoid an offence being committed. In other words, the shopkeeper must have a system in operation to avoid the commission of any offence, and that system must be effective.

Misleading price indications

Clearly, retailers are bound by the rules and to break them is a criminal offence, punishable on conviction or indictment (crown court) to an unlimited fine; and on summary conviction (magistrates' court) to a fine of up to the statutory maximum, which at present is £5,000.

In defining what it means by the word 'misleading', the 1987 Act covers the following five areas:

- indications about the actual price that the consumer will have to pay (for example, a retailer will commit an offence if he indicates a price for goods which is lower than the price he is actually going to charge)
- indications about any conditions attached to a price
- any indications about the way in which a price will be calculated
- indications about what is expected to happen to a price in future
- any indications concerning price comparisons.

Several defences are provided by the 1987 Act. These include: compliance with any applicable regulations approved by the Secretary of State for the purposes of the 1987 Act (generally speaking, none exist in relation to pricing at present); the defence of 'due diligence', namely, that the retailer has taken all reasonable steps and exercised all due diligence to avoid committing the offence; and other defences, such as that for a publisher or publishing agent.

Enforcement of the law on prices is placed on the local Trading Standards or Consumer Protection Departments and, as with the Trade Descriptions Act 1968, authority is given to make test purchases of goods, to enter business premises and to inspect any goods, and to seize and detain goods where appropriate. Power is also conferred to examine any procedure connected with the making of the goods. As before, failure to allow a Trading Standards Officer to carry out his legal duties is a criminal offence – namely that of obstruction.

Code of Practice for Traders on Price Indications (DTI Nov 1988)

The purpose of this code is to 'put the meat on the bones' of the pricing law by setting out what is good trading practice to follow, so helping the trader to avoid the pitfalls of giving a misleading price indication.

Compliance with the code is important since it has 'evidential status', which means that if a trader is taken to court for giving a misleading price indication, the court can take into account whether or not the trader has followed the code. If he or she has followed it, that will not be an absolute defence, but it will 'tend to show' that the trader has not committed an offence. Failure to follow the code may make it difficult for a trader to establish the 'due diligence' defence given to him by the 1987 Act.

The code covers a number of areas, each of which is important. In any comparison with the trader's own previous price:

- the previous price should be the *cost* price at which the product was available to consumers in the previous six months
- the product should have been available to consumers at that price for at least 28 consecutive days in the previous six months
- the previous price should have applied (as above) for that period at the *same* shop where the reduced price is now being offered.

Where these conditions are met, the price indication is unlikely to be misleading. Where the previous price in a comparison does not meet one or more of these conditions, the code provides appropriate guidelines on what the trader should do to avoid committing an offence. In these circumstances, the code requires the trader to give a clear and positive explanation of the period and the circumstances in which that higher price applied. The explanation must be displayed clearly, and as prominently as the price indication.

The following is an example of the kind of explanation envisaged by the code:

January Sale
£4.50
Previous price £9
from 10 to 31 December

Other examples of the kinds of explanation required are also given, such as: 'These goods were on sale here at the higher price from 1 February to 26 February', or 'These goods were on sale at the higher price in 10 of our 95 stores only'.

General disclaimers should not be used, and all comparisons shown should be fair and meaningful, and should always state the previous price as well as the lower price.

The code covers comparisons with recommended retail prices and other similar descriptions and defines a recommended retail price as meaning a price which has been recommended to the trader by the manufacturer or supplier as a price at which the product might be sold to consumers, that price not being significantly higher than prices at which the product is generally sold at the time the trader first makes that comparison, and there being a normal commercial relationship between the trader and the manufacturer or supplier. The code tells the trader that he or she must be dealing with the manufacturer or supplier on normal commercial terms.

In addition, the code expressly advises against the use of initials or abbreviations to describe the higher price in a comparison unless the trader uses the initials 'RRP' to describe a recommended retail price, or uses the abbreviation 'man. rec. price' to describe a manufacturer's recommended price.

The code states that all other descriptions should be written out in full, and shown clearly and prominently with the price indication. Other areas covered by the code include introductory offers, quoting a future price.

The code advises caution in describing offers as introductory offers, unless the trader intends to continue to offer the item for sale after the offer period is over, and to do so at a higher price. An introductory offer should only run for a reasonable period, otherwise it becomes misleading to describe it as introductory. By way of guidance, the code specifies that 'reasonable' relates to a 'matter of weeks, not months'. Further guidelines are that an offer is unlikely to be misleading if the trader states the date that the offer will end, and keeps to it. A trader who extends the offer period must make it clear that he has done so.

In providing guidance for a trader on what to do if he wants to quote a future price as part of the price comparison, the code advises that an 'after-sale' price or 'after promotion' price should only be used if the trader concerned is certain that he will continue to offer identical items at that price for at least 28 days in the three months after the end of the offer period, or after the offer stocks run out. Where a trader does quote a future price, he may not use initials such as 'ASP' or 'APP' to describe it. The code specifies that the words should be written out in full, and be clearly and prominently displayed with the price indication.

'Worth' and 'value' claims are also covered in the code of practice, and the trader is advised against comparing his prices with an amount of money described as 'worth' or 'value'. (For example, it would be in contravention of the code for a retailer to say: 'Worth £10, our price £5.')

Consult your local Trading Standards Department for advice on any of the requirements and, in turn, be prepared to co-operate with the Department and respond to its reasonable requests for information and assistance.

Copies of the code may be obtained free from the Consumer Affairs Division of the Department of Trade and Industry.

Further regulations on price indications

The Price Marking Order 1991 requires the selling price of goods offered to consumers to be indicated in writing. The Order applies to virtually all goods offered for retail sale. The main exceptions are goods sold in the course of the provision of a service, food sold and consumed in catering establishments, antiques and works of art.

The selling price can be shown on the goods themselves, on a ticket or notice near them or grouped together with other prices on a list in close proximity to the goods. The unit price must be shown for goods sold from bulk or pre-packed in quantity, and a price per pound or kilogram must be shown for most fruit and vegetables (although if a metric unit price is shown then an imperial unit price must be displayed in close proximity to it).

VAT must be included in the price if the customers are mainly private consumers, but VAT can be shown separately from the basic price if the trader is selling mostly to business customers. Additional charges which the customer has to pay, such as delivery, must be included in the price displayed or be shown with equal prominence.

There are special provisions relating to jewellery, precious metals, goods not on display and goods sold by mail order.

The Guidance Note for Price Indications (Method of Payment) Regulations 1991 concern retailers who charge different amounts for goods or services depending on the method of payment (e.g. adding a percentage for payment by credit card or a fee for payment by cheque). The trader must state the methods of payment to which any indicated price does not apply and must specify the difference between the marked price and any other price as a percentage or as an amount of money. This information must be given by notices placed at public entrances to the premises and at points of payment. Items may also be marked individually with two or more prices.

Penalties for failing to comply with either of the above regulations are, on summary conviction, a fine up to £5,000, or, on conviction on indictment, an unlimited fine. Enquiries should be addressed to Consumer Affairs Division, 2c, Room 320, Department of Trade and Industry, 10–18 Victoria Street, London SW1H 0NN TEL 071-215 3291.

Origin marking/place of production

Traders are required to state the origin of imported goods only if they are presented in a way which would give to consumers the impression that they were made in a particular place and were not, in fact, made there. The new legal duty, then, is to correct a misleading impression given as to place of production or manufacture. The use of a trade mark or of a particular language will not, in itself, attract the new legal requirement, but it may do so if the trade mark or use of language is likely to mislead.

Breach of this requirement is a criminal offence, punishable on summary conviction with a fine of up to £5,000, and on conviction on indictment with an unlimited fine, or up to two years' imprisonment, or both.

The Department of Trade and Industry has produced a set of guidance notes for traders on the law – the Trade Descriptions (Place of Production) (Marking) Order 1988. Copies are obtainable, free of charge, from the Department's Consumer Affairs Division.

The general safety requirement

In addition to its provisions on pricing and its repeal of the present law on origin marking, the Consumer Protection Act 1987 introduced a 'general safety requirement' for consumer goods supplied in the United Kingdom. Since 1 October 1987 it has been a criminal offence to supply consumer goods which are not reasonably safe. Penalties can result in a fine of not more than £5,000 per offence, or in up to six months' imprisonment, or both. The general safety requirement applies to anyone who deals in consumer goods which are not reasonably safe 'having regard to all the circumstances', and these circumstances include such aspects as the manner in which the goods are marketed; any warnings or instructions given with them; the means, if any, and the cost of making the goods safe; and any published safety standards for the goods in question. Various defences are available, including that the goods conform to any applicable safety regulations or safety standards approved by the Secretary of State. A register of safety standards for goods is available for public inspection at the Department of Trade and Industry Library at 1 Victoria Street, London SW1A 0ET. An important defence exists especially for the retailer, that he neither knew, nor had reasonable grounds for believing, that the goods failed to comply with the general safety requirement.

Enforcement of the general safety requirement is the responsibility of the local Trading Standards Departments, which have been given increased powers for this purpose. Not only may they seize goods which offend against the new requirement, but they may also issue suspension notices, so prohibiting suppliers from selling offending goods, and they may further apply to the courts for such goods to be made forfeit and subsequently destroyed.

Product liability

The Consumer Protection Act 1987 introduced into the United Kingdom the provisions of the European Community Directive on Product Liability. This brought into force the concept of strict liability (that is, liability without fault) for defective products. Under the 1987 Act, liability is channelled towards the producer, the importer and the own-brander of the product. In certain limited circumstances, other suppliers may be liable, and this could include the retailer.

Product liability is not restricted to consumer goods, and it has applied to products first supplied since 1 March 1988.

For further reading on this subject, you should obtain a copy of the *Guide to the Consumer Protection Act 1987 – Product Liability and Safety Provisions*, published free of charge by the Department of Trade and Industry, and obtainable from the Consumer Safety Unit of the Department of Trade and Industry, 10–18 Victoria Street, London SW1H 0NN   TEL 071-215 7877.

Giving customers credit for goods or services

As a business person, you are perfectly free to give credit to a customer for goods or services which you have supplied to him or her: that is, you can agree to allow him or her to defer payment. Or you may inform the customer that credit will not be available.

A creditor is not obliged to give a customer reasons for refusal, but if he or she has consulted a credit reference agency, the customer can demand to know the name and address of that agency – to enquire of it as to the information which it holds.

Consumer Credit Act 1974

The Consumer Credit Act 1974 and its subsequent Regulations set down the rules to be followed in dealing with credit – particularly in relation to licensing, credit references, credit cards or tokens, credit advertising, the giving of credit quotations and agreement forms for documenting credit transactions. You need to be aware of all these aspects and of how the law regulates credit agreements between business people and their customers.

The Consumer Credit Act 1974 regulates most of the agreements under which credit is advanced to any person (but not where credit is advanced to a limited company), regardless of whether the credit agreement is a hire purchase, a conditional sale or a credit agreement in respect of services rendered or goods supplied. It applies whether the person supplying the goods or services provides the credit facility or refers his or her customer to a finance house.

The Act imposes strict rules on advertising credit. It also gives customers the right to require a written quotation, clearly stating the exact terms on which credit is on offer. Although this right is rarely exercised, you need to know about it.

Consumer credit business

Any business which provides credit under credit agreements which are regulated by the 1974 Act is called a consumer credit business, for example a shop selling goods on its own credit terms or a finance house which supplies or finances goods under hire-purchase agreements.

Credit agreements

Before providing credit or hire facilities (such as, for example, renting out television sets or cars) you will need to ask your customer to sign an agreement, setting out his or her rights and obligations. In many circumstances, the customer has the right to cancel the agreement: if so, the agreement itself must contain a notice explaining the customer's legal rights. Certain provisions are in force which require various copies of the agreement to be given to the customer. You should be aware of them.

The Consumer Credit Act lays down detailed rules for the information to be given in an agreement form, and the statements of the customer's rights which must be shown.

Licences

Licensing is an essential part of the legal requirements on credit, and a person who carries on a consumer credit business must first obtain the appropriate credit licence. (If not, he or she commits a criminal offence.) The period during which a consumer credit licence has effect is now five years, but it can be varied, suspended or revoked by the Office of Fair Trading where the concept of 'fitness' is put in doubt.

There are currently six categories of credit licence, namely for:

- category A – consumer credit business
- category B – consumer hire business

- category C – credit brokerage
- category D – debt adjusting and debt counselling
- category E – debt collecting
- category F – credit reference agency.

A credit licence is not granted automatically, and each application is carefully vetted by the Office of Fair Trading. The Director General of Fair Trading must be satisfied that the prospective licence holder 'is a fit person to engage in activities covered by the licence' and that 'the name(s) under which he applies to be licensed is (or are) not misleading or otherwise undesirable'. Details of all licence applications are kept in a public register. If an application is turned down (which seldom happens), the shopkeeper can appeal. A right of appeal, on a point of law, can also be made to the courts.

The address to which you should apply for all credit licences is: The Office of Fair Trading, Consumer Credit Licensing Branch, Government Building, Bromyard Avenue, Acton, London W3 7BB TEL 071-242 2858. Licence application forms are also generally available from local authority Trading Standards Departments.

A shopkeeper will need to have a category A licence – which covers those situations where credit is offered to the customer. A shopkeeper without a licence who endeavours to enter into any credit agreement will not be able to enforce it against the debtor unless he or she obtains an order from the OFT permitting him or her to do so.

It will, in certain circumstances, be necessary for the shopkeeper to obtain a category C licence where he or she enters into 'credit brokerage'.

Credit brokerage business

Any business which introduces individuals who want credit to other businesses offering such facilities is a 'credit brokerage' business. So, if you do not sell a TV set on credit terms but refer your customer to a company which provides credit facilities, and handle the necessary paperwork, you are operating a credit brokerage business, and as such you must obtain a category C licence.

Canvassing

It is a criminal offence to canvass credit agreements for cash loans in people's homes unless the trader has a written invitation to visit, made before such facilities were discussed. Any trader who wishes to canvass credit agreements for the supply of goods and services off trade premises needs a special category of licence to permit this.

Further reading

Because consumer credit legislation is very intricate and involves so many regulations and calculations, you should obtain and read very carefully the information booklets, brochures and leaflets obtainable free of charge from the Office of Fair Trading, Room 306, Field House, 15–25 Bream's Buildings, London EC4A 1PR TEL 071-242 2858. They include: *Credit Charges* (how to calculate the total charge for credit and the annual percentage rate of charge); *Licensing* (describing the categories of consumer credit licence); *Advertisements and Quotations Regulations*; *Regulated and Exempt Agreements*; *Cancellable Agreements and Non-cancellable Agreements*; *Hire Agreements*; *Matters Arising During the Lifetime of an Agreement*.

The Consumer Credit Trade Association, Tennyson House, 159–165 Great Portland Street, London W1N 5FD   TEL 071-636 7564, publishes a series of short guides providing guidance on the Consumer Credit Act.

The Consumer Credit Trade Association also provides training to its members to meet requirements connected with all aspects of credit, and publishes detailed information on new legislation. It provides a personal advisory service and sells the standard documents complying with the Consumer Credit Act. Its members receive a bi-monthly journal, *Consumer Credit*. The annual membership fee for a new company is £164.50.

CHAPTER 13

SOME DREAMS EXPLORED

THERE ARE some businesses that have an enduring appeal for people hoping to become their own boss: having a bookshop; keeping a pub; being a newsagent. These seem to require no special training, and they bring you into contact with things which are generally associated with pleasure: alcoholic drink, magazines, tobacco, sweets, books.

An employment agency has the appeal of dealing with people, something which many people believe themselves to have a natural flair for.

Being a bookseller

Many people have a fantasy of keeping a bookshop because they like books. What is more, they may imagine that they will start off by selling, second-hand, all those surplus books now on their own shelves at home. The reality is not so.

An enthusiasm for books is not enough. Running a bookshop has its perils and pitfalls as well as its rewards. An understanding of retailing in general is essential, as well as a good knowledge of the way the book trade works, in order to make a success of running an independent bookshop at a time when the chain and multiple bookshops are growing in number and in strength.

Publishers offer the retailer set discount rates, which vary from publisher to publisher, and from book to book. Net profit in bookselling is notoriously low. Larger orders carry larger discounts, but it is a gamble to buy in a large number of copies on the chance of a potential bestseller. No bookseller can stock more than a fraction of the hundreds of thousands of titles in print.

Because of the Net Book Agreement, books by publishers who are signatories to the Agreement (most of them are) must be sold at the same 'net' price in all outlets, so price competition has traditionally not been a feature of the book trade. Instead, the emphasis has to be on service and stock. An independent bookseller needs to learn what to stock for the needs of the community he or she serves. Many independent bookshops are successful because they provide a good service, or devote themselves to specialising in a particular area (such as children's books, medical texts, history, cinema, etc).

The Booksellers Association of Great Britain and Ireland, 272 Vauxhall Bridge Road, London SW1V 1BA TEL 071-834 5477, offers advice, information and training. Joining will make it easier for you to open accounts with publishers, and will also allow you to participate in the Book Tokens Scheme (open to members only) and the Booksellers Clearing House, a central clearing facility which enables booksellers to pay a large number of publishers' monthly accounts in one single payment.

The Association also has available a number of publications aimed at new entrants to the trade, including the *Booksellers Association's Guide to Starting and Running a Bookshop*, aimed at people who wish to run their own business, and need to know all about the trade and the workings of a bookshop. The Association negotiates preferential rates for members on many essential services such as insurance and parcel delivery.

Keeping a pub

Not all publicans are self-employed, many are managers working for the brewery. To be self-employed, you must either own a free house or, more commonly, rent a public house from a brewery. For this, in the first place write to the brewery of your choice, ask for an interview and give details of yourself and your husband/wife, your experience in the licensed trade (if any) and the amount of capital that you have readily available for investment in the pub. The available capital would probably have to be between £10,000 and £30,000 to buy the stock and necessary equipment and give some working capital.

Breweries are selective about tenants, and prefer married couples who will work as a team. You are unlikely to be considered if you are over 55 years old. It is an advantage to have worked in the trade and have had some specific training, apart from general knowledge of retail business. It is not enough to have been a devoted customer. The address of the Brewers' Society is 42 Portman Square, London W1H 0BB   TEL 071-486 4831.

A pub has to be licensed by the local justices and if you become its tenant you have to apply to be named as the licensee. The application goes to the magistrates who hold licensing sessions at irregular intervals, about four times a year, but a protection order can be granted to give temporary authority to carry on the business until a new licence is granted.

If your application to be a tenant is accepted by the brewery, you will be required to enter into a tenancy agreement which, amongst other things, requires you to buy all your beers from the brewery, unless it is unable to supply a type of beer for which you can show demand on the part of your customers. The agreement may also require you to buy your wines, spirits, cider and minerals from the brewer, unless you can show that you are able to get them on more favourable terms elsewhere. All the profits on the sales of liquor and of food remain in your hands.

The work of a publican is hard and requires a capacity for appearing good humoured at all times, while keeping a sharp eye on both customers and staff; short-changing or overcharging customers, or giving friends double measures or cheap drinks is bad for business.

Being a newsagent, sweetseller, tobacconist

Running a small shop that sells mainly newspapers is not an easy life, nor outstandingly lucrative. Before you take over an existing shop, apart from the usual checks about the lease and the standing of the business, you must ensure that the wholesaler who is supplying the existing owner will continue to supply newspapers and magazines to you when you take over the shop. There is nothing automatic about this.

There may be a limitation on the number of papers that you are allowed to buy on sale or return, and some magazines are supplied on firm sale only. So you might find yourself with unsold stock.

You will need to stay open on every day on which newspapers appear, which is about 360 days of the year. Some newsagents, normally those who do not operate a delivery service, close on Sundays, but this makes for lost sales.

You must be up before the lark every day, taking delivery of papers and sorting them and marking them up if you operate delivery rounds. Among your headaches will be sending out bills to tardy customers, and explaining to customers why their newspaper or magazine has not arrived – which may be due to industrial action at the publishers or wholesalers.

If you do home deliveries, you must find schoolchildren to do your rounds and will have to deal with the local education authority inspectors. There are by-laws about employing children to deliver newspapers; children must be over 13 years old and you must be licensed by the local education authority and adhere to rules such as those about the weight of newspapers they may carry and that the rounds must be finished an hour before school starts.

Sweets and tobacco, being tempting, pocketable and anonymous, are readily stolen. Selling requires sharp-eyed vigilance both in the stock room and in the shop.

You will have to deal with numerous suppliers offering many lines, so that there will be the need for constant stock checks and reordering. This is where access to a computer might help, especially as the prices you are allowed to charge tend to change with surprising frequency.

It is not unusual for a newsagent to work a 90-hour week and do no better than just make a living.

An employment agency

It is important to realise that an employment agency is not easy money, and needs people who are willing to face quite tedious work, and have not only drive but also a vast amount of patience and good sales skills. It is necessary to have, or acquire, proper training in interviewing, backed by a good knowledge of the industry or area in which you intend to operate.

Before starting an agency, consider what type of agency you intend to open – office agency or secretarial and clerical staff plus probably temporary staff in the same categories; or a specialist agency, for example, computer staff, nursing staff, accountants, engineers. For specialists, it is important for at least one of the directors or partners to have a good knowledge and understanding of the types of jobs which occur in the particular area of work.

When planning to set up an agency, be sure to carry out adequate market research beforehand, because you will be operating in a highly competitive market. And do not make the mistake of thinking that you can run an employment agency in your spare time, after your ordinary day's work is finished.

Getting the clients

Building up contacts can be achieved by telephone or personal calls, or via literature about your business. Calls are likely to be better because the initiative is then yours, not the client's.

A small agency must build up personal contacts and operate on a personal basis but this cannot be rushed, and immediate first-name familiarity on the part of the agency is not always the way in.

It is important always to tell your client the truth about prospective candidates and not to hard-sell the applicant, so that the client will have confidence in your opinions on candidates, and will trust you – which is vitally important. It is no good sending unsuitable applicants to clients in the hope of doing business.

Recruiting the applicants

If your premises have a shop front, display the job vacancies for temporary and permanent staff in your windows. Alternatively, and in addition, it is a good idea to advertise permanent job vacancies in a local paper or, for specialist agencies, a national paper or specialist journals. The wording of the advert should aim to bring in not a quantity, but the right quality, of applicants: the type of candidates who can do the job that is advertised. If you keep a record and analyse your responses from different media, you may learn which are the best to use for a particular type of vacancy.

Money matters

If you have temporary workers, you will need a fair amount of capital because you pay the temporary staff straightaway at the end of each week (at an agreed fee per hour, tax and insurance deducted) and although the hourly charge to the client is more (by how much depends on the category of staff), payment from the client may not come in for several weeks.

For permanent staff, you charge an introduction fee of 10 to 15 per cent of the annual salary. But when you first start an agency, the people whom you place in permanent jobs sometimes do not start their employment immediately, which can result in something like six to eight weeks, or more, passing before you get paid any fees.

Formalities

A licence has to be obtained from the Department of Employment before you start. You have to complete an application form with a lot of personal information including the work history of all partners or directors of the proposed agency. You have to display a notice, which the Department of Employment lets you have, on the outside of the proposed offices and also put an advertisement with similar wording into the local papers, in case anybody wishes to raise any objection.

Until everything is cleared and a licence granted, it is illegal to carry on any business – so be careful not to sign any binding documents for the proposed offices, such as a lease. An outsider can raise objections to either the newspaper advertisement or the notice outside the proposed office, and if they are sustained by the Department, no licence is then granted.

Running an employment agency involves a great deal of record-keeping to comply with the Employment Agencies Act. There is probably enough record-keeping, paperwork and book-keeping to keep one person fully occupied.

It is also important to have a good broad knowledge of the various statutes and regulations concerning employers and employees.

The Federation of Recruitment and Employment Services Ltd., 36–38 Mortimer Street, London W1N 7RB TEL 071-323 4300, can give some preliminary advice on running a private recruitment consultancy, and will forward an information pack about the FRES on request. It is the trade association for the private recruitment service, and gives advice on terms of business, documentation, insurance and legal matters to its members.

The Institute of Employment Consultants, 6 Guildford Road, Woking, Surrey GU22 7PX TEL (0483) 766442, offers courses in employment consultancy and all aspects of agency work and sets examinations for recruitment specialists, including the Certificate in Recruitment Practice (operated jointly with the Associated Examining Board), as well as a correspondence course leading to a Foundation Vocational Award in employment agency practice. The IEC acts as an advisory body for recruitment specialists from a wide variety of fields.

CHAPTER 14

AN EXPORTER

A MANUFACTURER who has a product that is competitive in the UK market, but who is looking for another way of increasing business, may achieve the growth needed by selling goods abroad. At the same time the manufacturer will be spreading his or her risks, since even if there should be a world recession, it is unlikely that all countries will be equally affected, and being able to manufacture in larger batches may also make him or her more competitive on the home market.

It is also possible to export without manufacturing, by becoming an export merchant or export agent, and selling abroad goods bought from manufacturers in Britain.

You must pick your markets intelligently, and do some basic research to find out which countries are most likely to want to import what you have to sell, rather than trying to export bacon-flavoured crisps to the Middle East; or goods that are prohibited materials in another country according to their national regulations; or goods which do not comply with that country's standard specifications.

Selling abroad carries the same problems as the home trade – plus some others, such as: arranging the packing and shipment of goods to countries perhaps half a world away; complying with a great variety of foreign import regulations; securing payment in a world of shifting currency values and methods of payment. The exporter must be ready to cope with the unforeseen at home (such as a dock strike) and abroad (such as a revolution).

Exporting is not something you can fit into the odd moments you can spare from other concerns. If you plan to manufacture for sale both at home and abroad, either directly or through agents, you will need staff trained to deal with all aspects of exporting.

If your resources do not run to this, you might do better to sell overseas through an export intermediary – an export merchant, an export manager, or a buying house representing overseas importers, while you concentrate on building up the manufacturing side of your business and developing your domestic market. The British Exporters Association (BExA) can assist you in contacting appropriate intermediaries – commonly called export houses – through its *Directory of Export Buyers in the UK* (£78 including postage and packing) and the periodic *Export Enquiry Circular* in which, for a nominal charge, you can place a notice detailing your product. This will then be seen by all the Association's export house members, and those interested will contact you direct. The British Exporters Association estimates the cost of setting up your own competent export department at some £60,000. But it need cost you nothing to use an export house.

When your export business is on a firm footing, you can gradually build up your own export unit: for instance, by employing part-time, retired export specialists, and by training existing staff. The Institute of Export provides an Export Specialists service, and education and training in exporting.

There is yet another way to export: British confirming houses are constantly placing orders with UK manufacturers on behalf of their overseas principals or buyers. A confirming house will pay a supplier on shipment, and will, if necessary, extend credit for up to 180 days to the overseas importer. You must register your willingness to act as a supplier with appropriate confirming houses: their names can be obtained from BExA's *Directory of Export Buyers in the UK* (see above), or from the *Directory of Export Buyers in the UK*, published at £78 by Trade Research Publications, 6 Beech Hill Court, Gravel Path, Berkhamsted, Herts HP4 2PR   TEL (0442) 863951.

If you plan to become an export merchant or agent yourself, you will be wise to start with only one or two kinds of goods. Make yourself thoroughly familiar with them, and do not extend your range until you are well established in the trade.

Exporting, step by step

Most of the basic steps are the same whether you are dealing with goods manufactured by yourself or by some other firm.

Deciding where to export

Your first inkling of a possible market may already have come to you, in the shape of unsolicited enquiries from abroad; or friends in the trade may have mentioned some possible opening. From these, and sources such as the trade press and newspapers, you can pick out one or two possible markets; then you need to do some desk research to find out the most hopeful. The DTI/FCO joint Overseas Trade Services (OTS) operation offers a wide range of help, advice and support at each stage of the export process. Your first point of contact for advice on what is available should be the Department of Trade and Industry's regional offices, Scottish Trade International, the Welsh Office Industry Department or the Industrial Development Board for Northern Ireland. In addition, there are market branches, which provide information on particular countries, such as duties, local taxes, exchange controls.

The Export Market Information Centre (EMIC), formerly the Statistics and Market Intelligence Library, is provided by the OTS to help British exporters in carrying out desk research. It holds a variety of information on overseas markets. Sources available include overseas statistical publications, foreign trade and telephone directories, some market surveys of overseas markets, and mail order catalogues and development plans.

For EMIC's address, see DTI address page 24. The staff cannot carry out research on your behalf, but will help you with advice on sources.

Through its Market Information Enquiry Service, OTS offers a tailor-made service provided by FCO commercial posts overseas, which answers specific questions about the opportunities for products, processes and services in overseas markets.

Looking at your product

When you have found one or two markets that look promising, make sure that your product or service fits the needs of those markets. A number of organisations can provide you with information free of charge or at subsidised rates: Overseas Trade Services, in addition to its London headquarters, has a network of regional offices throughout the United Kingdom. Through these you can obtain commercial information from diplomatic service posts. OTS also publishes a range of export publications giving background information on a specific market or a more detailed look at the opportunities for particular products or services within that market. Prices start at £5 and a catalogue can be obtained by telephoning (0789) 299096.

Other sources are Chambers of Commerce, foreign diplomatic posts in London, the trade press, and the business sections of the national press. You should also contact an organisation called Technical Help to Exporters (part of British Standards Institution), Linford Wood, Milton Keynes, Bucks MK14 6LE TEL (0908) 220022, for advice on technical requirements for products in foreign countries: some of the services it offers are free, others are charged for. A leaflet giving all the details is available on request.

Developing the market

Amongst the services offered is help towards the cost of overseas market research through the Export Marketing Research Scheme (this scheme is operated by the ABCC on behalf of the DTI), and financial support if you join a trade mission going abroad or participate in an overseas trade fair or exhibition. It also helps firms to display their products there. It can also help promote new and innovative products overseas through its new products from Britain service.

OTS' Export Intelligence Service notifies UK business of overseas opportunities. Sales leads are identified from a variety of sources including Foreign and Commonwealth Office commercial staff overseas. These opportunities are made available to subscribers of a matching service run by Prelink Ltd or to those who access the data remotely on a database operated by FT Profile. Details can be obtained from your nearest office.

By correspondence and by visits to the markets, you should try to find channels of distribution; these can vary from direct sales to individual outlets, to having your own marketing company. There will probably be companies with established operations who are prepared to help you, for agreed terms.

OTS recommends that you find a good agent in each market (and will help you with this through its Export Representative Service) and then give the agent full back-up support. OTS can also provide, through its Overseas Status Report Service, a report on the local standing probity, and representational capacity of overseas companies. You will need to develop suitable promotional material. If it is to be in a foreign language, it should be prepared by a native speaker who also has some relevant technical knowledge.

It is important to have a watertight agreement with each overseas agent. The Institute of Export, Export House, 64 Clifton Street, London EC2A 4HB TEL 071-247 9812, may be able to help.

Securing a profit

To ensure a profit from overseas sales, it is important to have reliable channels of distribution. So take professional advice: from a freight forwarder, about the terms on which you should trade; from a broker, about insurance; from the international division of your bank, about handling payment. You may also need to secure yourself against credit risks, for example, through the ECGD (the Export Credits Guarantee Department), but if you can, avoid taking such risks when you first start to export. Many overseas buyers expect credit, therefore risks cannot be entirely avoided. By insuring the credit risk, exporters can ask banks or other financial institutions for non-recourse finance, from the date of shipment.

Managing the operation

It is unlikely that anyone will place an order without first receiving a quotation. To save time, send this promptly in the form of a pro-forma invoice.

A pro-forma invoice looks like an ordinary invoice, except for the words 'pro-forma' in the heading. The figures you quote are binding. The invoice should indicate the type and quantity of goods, with details of their prices, the delivery time, the terms of payment (such as letter of credit or sight draft), the currency in which the deal is to be made, the method of packing. It should also state whether the prices quoted are as defined under INCO (United Nations inter-governmental consultative organisation) terms as, for example:

f.a.s.	– free alongside ship price includes delivery to the docks (named port)
f.o.b.	– free on board at named port price includes delivery on board ship
DCP (or C&F)	– cost and freight or carriage (paid to . . .) price includes freight charges, but not insurance charges, to a named port of destination
CIP	– cost, freight or carriage insurance (paid to . . .) price includes both freight and insurance charges to an agreed port of destination.

All the terms should be clearly set out in the quotation or pro-forma invoice, because once the customer has signified his or her acceptance of this, it becomes a contract binding on both parties. Hence, you should also state how long your offer remains valid. If an order has been confirmed by the customer by telex, it is necessary to get confirmation by letter; pro-forma invoices must also be sent by mail.

Dealing with suppliers

Unless you are the manufacturer of the goods, or have them in stock when you receive an enquiry, you will need to contact the manufacturers or stockists for quotations. You must emphasise that the goods will have to be suitably packed for export. The suppliers' quotations or pro-forma invoices should be with prices quoted f.o.b. or DCP or CIP, as requested.

If a supplier will only quote f.o.b., you must ask for an approximate shipping specification: the number of packages, cartons, cases, etc. that will be needed, the delivery time, their gross and net weights and their shipping measurements. You need this information to estimate the cost of freight, and insurance if required, plus the shipping expenses which the forwarding agents will charge. Your supplier's terms of payment may be cash with order or cash within seven days from receipt of invoice (possibly with a special cash discount); or monthly account (subject to satisfactory trade and bank references); or some other method of payment.

Be very meticulous in comparing your supplier's quotation with the pro-forma invoice you send to your potential customer overseas. Any discrepancies between the supplier's descriptions and the customer's requirements must be sorted out because, once the order is placed, the customer will usually insist on receiving the goods exactly as specified in the pro-forma invoice. Any confusion about whether the prices quoted are f.o.b., DCP or CIP can play havoc with the calculations of an exporter's profit.

Croner's Reference Book for Exporters contains a wealth of information about all aspects of the export trade, with separate entries for every country, giving a summary of its individual import regulations. Use it to check that your freight forwarder is giving you good advice. It is a loose-leaf book, and its price includes a year's updating amendments. There is also an annual amendments subscription.

Arrangements for shipment

For sending goods by sea or air you will normally need the services of a freight forwarder, who should be a registered trading member of BIFA, the British International Freight Association. The freight forwarder will advise you on the best method of transportation to your destination, depending on your requirements as to speed, safety and cost, and will quote for the cost of freight and other charges, prepare most of the shipping and customs documents, arrange marine insurance, if required, and attend to other shipping details.

When the goods have gone forward to the ship, the forwarder will obtain bills of lading – detailed receipts for the goods, issued by the shipping company, and containing a contract whereby the company undertakes to deliver the goods to a specified port of destination.

The bill of lading is the most important part of the transaction, being a document of title to the goods listed in it, but is now increasingly superseded by the non-negotiable sea waybill, which is not a document of title; it enables the consignee to clear the goods without acquiring a title to them.

In the deep-sea liner trade, goods are now generally moved in containers, which may contain several different consignments, and be packed inland, before being moved to the docks. Goods to short-sea destinations, such as the Continent, are usually moved on road vehicles straight on to the ferries ('ro ro' movements). All this allows a more rapid distribution of goods.

Forwarding freight by air

The procedure is similar to that for shipping, with these differences: the goods are usually collected by the air freight forwarder and taken into his or her premises prior to being delivered to the airline sheds at the airport. Many forwarders will give quotations on a door-to-door basis. The document of carriage is called an air waybill, and is not a document of title.

The British International Freight Association will supply the names of registered freight forwarders, both for shipping and air freight (E2), as well as a booklet, *A Brief Introduction to Freight Forwarding*.

A particularly rapid way of sending goods by air is through the use of express air services; these are overnight carriers who deal directly with exporters, use simple documentation, and arrange for goods to be cleared through customs.

Exporting by post (international parcels)

If the goods you are exporting are neither bulky nor heavy, it may be preferable to send them by air parcel post directly to the customers. The procedure is simple: you complete the appropriate customs declaration forms (obtainable from the post office) and hand them in when posting the parcel in the usual way. Your payment terms could be CBD (cash before delivery) or COD (cash on delivery). Every country has its own regulations as to customs declaration forms, packing and prohibited goods. Consult the staff at your nearest main post office at the time of despatching each consignment. Other information is available from your local representative of the International Parcels division of the Post Office.

Customs

The exporter/manufacturer bears full responsibility for the declaration of the correct commodity code for the goods, and for the customs declaration, even though the forms may have been completed by someone else – the freight forwarder acting as the agent, or any other person.

Calculating your prices

In order to calculate the price to your customer abroad, you must have the following items of information:

- the amount of any discounts for cash or quantity that your supplier will allow you (unless you are exporting your own goods)
- any on-costs for export packing
- cost of freight and transportation expenses; your forwarding agent will calculate these for you
- bank charges; imposed by the bank through which you receive payment (between 12.5 per cent and 25 per cent of the total invoice value)
- any costs for currency exchange
- insurance cost for CIP quotations; you must also allow for the cost of insurance for the goods in transit from the works, factory or store in this country to the docks if this is not included in the supplier's price; in some cases you may need a seller's interest policy even for an f.o.b. quote; you may need to add an ECGD premium
- commission for your agent abroad, if you have one
- your own profit.

Insurance

You will need to find a reputable insurance company, probably through an insurance broker, to insure all your shipments. The insurers should supply you with a list of tariffs for different countries and types of risk. They will require information about each individual consignment, and will then quote accordingly. Some Middle Eastern countries have their own insurance companies, and ask for the goods to be shipped DCP only.

A consignment is generally insured up to the moment it is claimed by the consignee, including any time spent in a warehouse overseas: but, because of the high risk of pilferage, insurance companies may refuse to insure cargoes bound for some destinations beyond the time of arrival.

Payment for exports

The most commonly employed methods of payment for export orders are as follows:

Cash with order/cash before delivery
This is the most desirable method. You may not get it, but you can always ask.

Documentary letter of credit
With this method the exporter receives payment from a bank after presenting a complete set of documents precisely conforming to the requirements of the credit within the time limit specified in the credit.

The customer, having accepted your quotation, opens a letter of credit in your favour: that is, he or she instructs the bank abroad to instruct a bank in Britain to pay you the agreed amount, on production of a correct and complete set of documents (hence 'documentary') and on satisfying any other agreed conditions.

There are several types of letter of credit (L/C for short). The most desirable is an irrevocable letter of credit confirmed (i.e., underwritten) by a recognised bank in Britain. Payment is guaranteed in all circumstances – revolution, currency crash, insolvency, act of God included. This type of L/C is the hardest of all to come by.

There are also unconfirmed irrevocable credits, the terms of which cannot be varied, save by agreement, and revocable letters of credit, which may facilitate payment, but are not secure. Use these when the importer is trustworthy, and his country's exchange controls require an L/C.

Forwarding documents

The complete set of documents required will be listed in the bank's advice of the credit, and may include:

- the original letter of credit
- the exporter's commercial invoice, signed (not the pro-forma, although it contains the same information)
- the bill of lading: two originals, endorsed in the form demanded by the bank, signed, dated and stamped 'shipped on board' by the shipping company, plus three or more non-negotiable copies; or a receipted waybill.
- the insurance policy or certificate, in duplicate
- a set of two bills of exchange or a sight draft (which are a demand for payment)
- a certificate of origin (issued and certified by a designated UK Chamber of Commerce) specifying the origin of the goods. Details of designated Chambers in UK may be obtained from the Association of British Chambers of Commerce.
- export and import licences
- inspection certificates
- health certificates
- consular invoices.

Whether or not all these documents are specified in the letter of credit, many of them will be required, in any case, by the buyer, for import purposes.

All the documents must conform in every particular to the requirements of the letter of credit and to the customer's order with regard to the type and quantity of the goods, the marks (which identify the goods) and the measurements of the packing cases.

If there are any discrepancies, the bank is likely to withhold payment. And since the customer will be unable to claim the goods until the documents arrive at his or her end (forwarded by the bank), he or she may have to pay demurrage – the cost of storing them in a warehouse – for which the customer will want to be reimbursed by the exporter.

Many document presentations are rejected because the documents are incorrect, or late, or both. Your recourse in such a case is to send a set of correct documents if time allows; if not, ask the bank to telex the customer for permission to pay in spite of error or lateness.

Do not send the documents to the customer's bank if they have already been rejected; and do not give the bank indemnity against payment. This takes a long time, and you will be charged interest.

Payment against documentary collection

This method should be used only with a tried and proven customer. The customer, in turn, must trust the exporter to supply goods of the exact type and quantity ordered: he or she undertakes to pay on a specified date (usually the arrival of the documents at the bank overseas or, in practice, on the arrival of the goods at the destination). The terms of payment should be specified. If goods are exported without an explicit arrangement to an unknown or unreliable customer, the exporter may be in a situation where there is a loss of control of the goods without any certainty of receiving payment.

The same documents as for a letter of credit are required. The bank will release the documents to the customer (thus enabling him or her to claim the goods) when it has collected the payment.

Payment by 30, 60 or 90 days drafts

This is a method which grants credit to the customer. It should be extended only to known customers in good financial standing. Before the customer can claim the documents, he or she must sign the drafts or bills of exchange, which you have issued, promising to pay the money due at some stated date – usually in 30, 60 or 90 days. The customer is then given the documents and can collect the goods – and sell them before having to pay for them. In EC countries, some banks will avalise (guarantee) payment by their customers of bills of exchange.

Since you will receive your money with some delay, a reasonable allowance for interest should have been included in the price.

Before quoting payment terms which do not guarantee payment, always check the credit rating of your customer, and use debt collectors if you are not paid in a reasonable time.

Bank overdraft has been the exporter's traditional method of filling the gap between shipment and payment, but now short-term export finance is available from several sources, to help exporters with payment delays and foreign exchange fluctuations. Midland Bank, Barclays Bank and National Westminster Bank all have export finance schemes. You would be paid 80 to 90 per cent of the insured value of the goods at the time of shipment.

Protection against export risks

ECGD, the United Kingdom's official export credit insurer, is a government department designed to protect the exporter against some of the hazards of trading overseas. ECGDs Insurance Services Group was privatised in December 1991. Insurance is available on this basis through a broker or NCH (UK) Credit Insurance, Cardiff (0222) 824000 or Trade Indemnity in London and other private insurance companies.

ECGD customers can choose whether to insure all or part of their exports: cover can be tailored to fit particular customers' needs. Protection can be given not only to goods but also to a wide range of invisible earnings, such as consultancy, royalty payments and leasing agreements.

UK merchants and exporters who trade in foreign goods or commodities between other countries can benefit from ECGD's insurance cover for such external trade. This 'multi-sourcing' is likely to grow in importance.

Cover normally starts from the date of shipment. But exporters of capital goods who need a period for construction in the UK can start the insurance cover from when the contract is signed.

An ECGD policy may generally be used to finance exports from the time of shipment. Most banks and financial institutions should accept the policy as suitable collateral for such borrowings. The policy thus allows exporters to grant their overseas customers credit, which may clinch the order.

Individual applications for credit limits for particular customers overseas are agreed quickly: more than half are decided within 24 hours of receipt in ECGD's offices.

Private credit insurance is also available, and has fewer restrictions to insurance cover, plus the advantage of being able to combine export and domestic cover under the terms of one policy. There are several private insurers, the largest of which is Trade Indemnity plc, 12–34 Great Eastern Street, London EC2A 3AX   TEL 071-739 4311.

Exporting through confirming houses

Some British export houses (confirming houses) act on behalf of overseas customers. Instead of dealing with the ultimate customer, the exporter deals with the confirming house, and presents the usual shipping documents to it. The ECGD can give insurance for such transactions if there is any giving of export credit involved.

Some confirming houses charge the exporter a small commission for their services, others are paid by the customer.

Some useful addresses for exporters

Association of British Chambers of Commerce, Sovereign House, 9 Tufton Street, London SW1P 3QB   TEL 071-222 1555

British Exporters Association, 16 Dartmouth Street, London SW1H 9BL   TEL 071-222 5419

British International Freight Association (incorporating the Institute of Freight Forwarders), Redfern House, Browells Lane, Feltham, Middlesex TW13 7EP   TEL 081-844 2266

Department of Trade and Industry (British Overseas Trade Board), Bridge Place, 88–89 Eccleston Square, London SW1V 1PT   TEL 071-215 0574

ECGD, 2 Exchange Tower, Harbour Exchange Square, London E14 9JS   TEL 071-512 7000

SITPRO (The Simpler Trade Procedures Board), 2nd Floor, 29 Glasshouse Street, London W1R 5RG   TEL 071-287 3525

CHAPTER 15

Bankruptcy

IF YOUR financial position deteriorates so much that you are unable to pay your unsecured debts, or where it appears that there is no reasonable prospect that you will be able to pay a debt in the future, when it falls due for payment, a creditor may, if you owe him or her at least £750, bring bankruptcy proceedings against you. Two or more creditors may act jointly. The creditor has to serve on you a formal demand, requiring you:

- to pay the debt, *or*
- to give security for it, *or*
- to compound for the petition debt: in other words, to propose an arrangement with the petitioning creditor, so that the debt can be paid off under an agreed scheme of payments.

If the debt is a future debt, the demand will require you to establish to the reasonable satisfaction of the creditor that you will be able to pay the debt when it falls due.

If you do not comply with the demand, or make an application to a bankruptcy court (the High Court in London or certain specified county courts) to set aside the demand (for example on the grounds that the money is not due, or that you have a claim against the creditor that equals or exceeds your debt to him), the creditor may, after the expiration of twenty-one days (or even earlier in exceptional cases) file a bankruptcy petition in a bankruptcy court.

The bankruptcy petition will be endorsed with the day and time of the hearing, and must be served on you by a process server in the first instance – but should the process server fail in several attempts to serve the petition, the court may give permission for a substituted service – that is, the post – to be used.

There is another way for a creditor to start bankruptcy proceedings (though a petition for bankruptcy is still required). When a debt is payable immediately, and the creditor can show the court that execution (or other process issued in respect of the debt on a judgment or order of any court) has been returned unsatisfied in whole or in part – perhaps because there are no funds – that creditor may ask the court for a bankruptcy order.

The court has a discretion whether or not to make a bankruptcy order on the petition but will probably do so unless you:

- have paid off the debt
- can show that the debt is not due
- can show that there are sums owed to you by the creditor, which equal or exceed the debt due to him or her
- can show that you have made a proposal to compound or secure the debt, and that the creditor has unreasonably refused such proposal
- if the debt is a future debt, can satisfy the court that there is a reasonable prospect that you will be able to pay the debt when it falls due.

The court has power to adjourn or stay the petition, and might do so to enable you to make proposals to secure or compound the debt, or to pay it off, possibly by instalments. The court has a duty to protect the interest of all creditors and the public generally, and it may well not adjourn or stay the petition unless it is satisfied that you could deal not only with the petitioning creditor's debt but also with all your other unsecured debts.

Avoiding bankruptcy proceedings

If you are in a situation where you cannot pay your debts in full, you may prefer to take steps yourself rather than allow a creditor to start bankruptcy proceedings against you. One step would be to write informally to all your creditors, asking them to agree to accept payments according to a schedule agreed with them all. This has the advantage of cheapness, but will only work if all your creditors agree, and still leaves you liable to bankruptcy proceedings if any one of them changes his or her mind.

Administration order

If your debts are less than £5,000 and there is a county court judgment for at least one of the debts, you can apply to that court for an administration order to be made. Such an order will provide for all your debts (whether or not there are court orders relating to them) to be paid by single weekly or monthly payments to the court. The court will accumulate the payments and distribute them to your creditors pro rata, from time to time. Provided that you keep up such payments, no steps can be taken to enforce the debts by other means.

If you have no prospect of paying off all your debts within a reasonable time, the court can, on your application, order that you pay only a limited percentage of your debts.

Voluntary arrangement with creditors

The Insolvency Act 1986 provides for voluntary arrangements to be made with your creditors, by enabling you to apply for approval of a composition or scheme whereby your debts are cleared by an offer to creditors made with the assistance of an insolvency practitioner.

After seeing an insolvency practitioner, you must first of all apply to the court for an interim order, stating in your application that you intend to make a proposal to creditors for a voluntary arrangement. In your application you must name a qualified insolvency practitioner who will help you to prepare the proposal for a voluntary arrangement. The local bankruptcy court will have a list of insolvency practitioners. If the court then makes an interim order, this will have the effect, during the period for which it is in force, of stopping any other proceedings, execution or other legal process from being commenced or continued against you or your property without the leave of the court.

No bankruptcy petition relating to you may be presented or proceeded with while the interim order is in force. The insolvency practitioner will then report to the court on your proposal for a voluntary arrangement, having normally first discussed the position with you fully at an interview. If the court is then satisfied, following the insolvency practitioner's report, that a meeting of your creditors should be summoned to consider his proposal, the court will direct that the period of the interim order be extended, and creditors will be given the opportunity to consider the proposal at a meeting. If over 75 per cent in value of the creditors present and voting at the meeting, either in person or by proxy, approve the proposal, it will be binding on all creditors who were notified of it. The named insolvency practitioner, or another chosen by creditors, will then supervise the arrangement. If such an arrangement is then made and honoured, you will avoid bankruptcy and the restrictions and publicity which go with it.

The first step is to apply to a bankruptcy court for an interim order which, if made, prevents any bankruptcy proceedings being taken against you without the leave of the courts, or any other steps taken to enforce the judgment for a period of fourteen days (which can be extended). The insolvency practitioner has to enquire into your debts and consider whether a meeting of your creditors should be called to decide whether to agree to your proposals as to payment. If it is considered that such a meeting is worthwhile, he or she is responsible for calling the meeting. The creditors who come to the meeting decide whether or not to accept your scheme. If it is accepted, that decision binds any creditor who had notice of and was entitled to attend that meeting. You must then carry out your part of the scheme by making regular payments as agreed and abide by whatever else you are required to do.

If your creditors do not approve the scheme, then the interim order will lapse and any creditors can take steps to enforce the debt or start bankruptcy proceedings.

Own bankruptcy petition

Finally, you may present your own petition in bankruptcy on payment of £135 fee and deposit to the court. Such a petition must be accompanied by a statement of your affairs, with details of all your debts and assets on a form provided by the court. Where your unsecured debts are less than £20,000 and your assets total at least £2,000, the court may not make but may apply an immediate bankruptcy order, but may appoint an insolvency practitioner to report on a possible voluntary arrangement with creditors, if it appears appropriate to the court to do so. Where a bankruptcy order is made, a certificate of summary administration will only be issued where on the hearing of a debtor's petition it appears to the court that the unsecured liabilities are less than £20,000 and that within the period of five years ending with the presentation of the petition, the debtor has neither been adjudged bankrupt, nor made a composition with the creditors in satisfaction of his or her debts, or a scheme of arrangement of his affairs.

Effect of bankruptcy order

The effect of a bankruptcy order is that all your assets (subject to very limited exceptions) are vested in your trustee in bankruptcy on his appointment, and until then come under the control of the official receiver in bankruptcy. Your assets include your home, and the trustee can seek an order for possession (if it is owned solely by you) or possession and sale (if it is owned jointly). The court must take into account the rights of your spouse under the Matrimonial Homes Act 1983 in considering whether or not to make such an order, but once one year has elapsed from the date of the trustee's appointment, the court assumes (save in exceptional circumstances) that the rights of the creditors outweigh all other considerations.

Unless you have been bankrupt previously or the court otherwise orders, you normally remain bankrupt for three years (two years in the case of a certificate of summary administration) and you are then discharged from the disabilities of a bankrupt.

On discharge, your assets in the bankruptcy remain vested in your trustee, who is able to sell them to pay off your debts, and they remain so vested in the trustee until all your debts are paid in full and the bankruptcy order is annulled.

Although the discharge releases you from most of your bankruptcy debts, you remain liable for certain debts including any judgment for damages arising out of an action in negligence for personal injury, and any court orders in family proceedings, such as maintenance.

During the course of your bankruptcy you have a duty to complete a statement of affairs, giving full details of your debts and assets and also to assist the official receiver and your trustee in ascertaining your assets and getting them in. You may be required to attend a public examination, at which you will be questioned about the reasons for your insolvency and your dealing with assets. Your trustee may apply to the court for an order requiring you to make regular payments out of your income towards payment of your debts. You may be committing an offence if you fail to disclose your assets fully, or otherwise fail to co-operate with the trustee.

Under the Insolvency Act 1986, it is a criminal offence not to have kept proper accounting records of your business from a date two years prior to the presentation of the petition in bankruptcy, up to the date of the bankruptcy order or, having kept such books, not to have preserved them. The accounting records must be such as will show and explain the transactions of your business, and must include records of all cash received and paid; and, where the business deals in goods, there must be statements of annual stocktaking, and accounts of all goods sold and bought, showing (except for retail sales) the names of buyers and sellers. It is also an offence if, during the same period, you have materially contributed to or increased the extent of your insolvency by gambling or rash and hazardous speculation.

The principal disabilities of a bankrupt are that he or she commits an offence if he or she obtains, either alone or jointly, credit for more than £250 without disclosing the bankruptcy; or engages in business under a name other than that in which he or she was made bankrupt, without disclosing to the people with whom he or she is trading, the name in which he or she was made bankrupt.

Under the Company Directors Disqualification Act 1986 it is an offence (except with the court's permission) for a bankrupt either to act as a director or to be concerned in the promotion, formation or management of a limited company.

You can obtain a Guide to Bankruptcy from the DTI's Insolvency Service, Bridge Place, 88–89 Eccleston Square, London SW1V 1PT   TEL 071-215 0753.

INDEX